TREASURY OF LITERATURE

PRACTICE BOOK

EMERALD FOREST

HARCOURT BRACE & COMPANY
Orlando Atlanta Austin Boston San Francisco Chicago Dallas New York
Toronto London

CONTENTS

For permission to reprint copyrighted material, grateful acknowledgment is made to the following sources:

Atheneum Publishers, an imprint of Macmillan Publishing Company: From *The Gold Coin* by Alma Flor Ada. Text copyright © 1991 by Alma Flor Ada.

Harcourt Brace & Company: Entry for "wolf" from *HBJ School Dictionary,* Third Edition. Text copyright © 1990 by Harcourt Brace & Company.

Printed in the United States of America

ISBN 0-15-301295-1

12 13 14 15 16 054 01 00 99

• • • MIRETTE ON THE HIGH WIRE • • •

Name_____

Welcome to the circus! Each word below fits a clue that one of the circus dogs is holding. Write each word on the correct dog's sign.

> boardinghouse   acrobats   protégée
> retired   agent   balanced   wavering

They are performers who do stunts.
_____

someone whose training or career is helped by another person
_____

The wire walker
_____
on one foot.

a person who handles business for someone else
_____

a person who is no longer working
_____

This is the place to stay.
_____

moving back and forth unsteadily
_____

Use the words above to play a game. Write each word on two cards. Mix up the cards and spread them out face down. Pick two cards at a time. If they don't match, put them back. If they do match, use the word in a sentence and keep the cards. Take turns with a partner, and see who can collect the most cards.

••• MIRETTE ON THE HIGH WIRE •••

Name_____

A. One way to summarize a story is to complete a
character chart. Finish the chart below to describe Bellini.

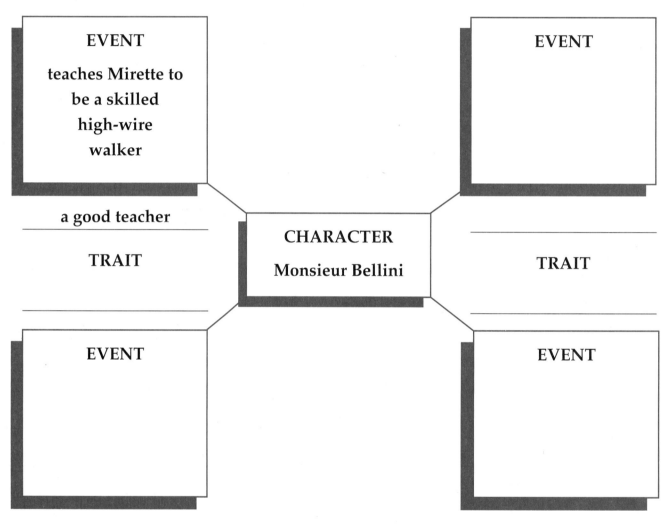

EVENT

teaches Mirette to
be a skilled
high-wire
walker

a good teacher
_____

TRAIT

_____

EVENT

CHARACTER

Monsieur Bellini

TRAIT

EVENT

EVENT

B. Write a brief summary statement of "Mirette on the High Wire."
Be sure to include information about Mirette as well as Bellini.

_____

_____

_____

Name_____

A. Read the paragraph below. Write *S* after each sentence
that makes a statement, and *Q* after each question.
Write *C* after each sentence that gives a command, and
F after each sentence that expresses a strong feeling.

What nerve it must take to be a circus performer! _____

What traits do you think you would need to have? _____

You would certainly need good coordination and very strong

muscles. _____ Start training now! _____

B. Rewrite each sentence so that it begins and ends correctly.

many performers practice for hours each day

_____

how can trapeze artists catch each other in mid-air

_____

wow, they must have strong arms

_____

Write about a remarkable performance you have seen or
done. Use at least two different kinds of sentences.

_____

_____

SUMMARIZING
the **L**EARNING A declarative sentence makes a _____. An
interrogative sentence asks a _____. An imperative sentence
makes a _____ or gives a command. An exclamatory sentence
expresses a _____ feeling.

••• MIRETTE ON THE HIGH WIRE •••

Name_____

Read the postcard to Bellini.

> *Dear Bellini,*
>
> *Remember our days with the circus, when we would walk on the high wire? How the crowds would cheer! Sadly, I am retired now. I am afraid of the wire! I wish someone could help me conquer my fear.*
>
> *Your old friend,*
> *Pierre*

What do you predict Bellini's answer will be?
Write it on the postcard.

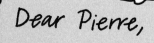

> *Dear Pierre,*
>
> _____
> _____
> _____
> _____
>
> *Your true friend,*
> *Bellini*

Now, read the postcard to Mirette on the next page.

Name_____

Dear Mirette,
    Guess what! I'm taking violin lessons! I love to play, but everyone says it's too hard for me. They say I'll never learn. What do you think?

Your cousin,
Marie

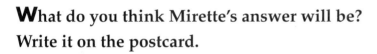

What do you think Mirette's answer will be?
Write it on the postcard.

Dear Marie,
_____
_____
_____
_____

Your cousin,
Mirette

What do you think will happen next to Mirette and Bellini? With a group of classmates, write a sequel to "Mirette on the High Wire." You might like to write your story in the form of a play and present it to another group.

MIRETTE ON THE HIGH WIRE

Name ___Kelsey McArthur___

Kevin is having trouble using the reading strategies you have learned. Help him put them to work! Read the story on this page. Then fill in the chart showing how you would use the strategies. The first one has been done for you.

THE NEW STAR

"You'll be rich! You'll be famous!" the agent told the young Suzette. "In all my years of working with circus performers, I've never seen anyone who can fly through the air on the trapeze as you do."

Suzette felt very shy and a little bit sad. It was true that she loved the trapeze, but she liked performing close to her home in southern France. Now the agent wanted her to perform in England and Italy!

"I don't want to go," she said softly.

The agent looked at her in amazement. "But you must!" he cried. "You are the new star! People will love you! When I close my eyes, I can just hear them cheering!"

Suddenly Suzette knew what she had to do. She stood up and looked straight at the agent. "I'm sorry," she said. "It would be nice to be a star, but it wouldn't make up for missing my home and my family and friends. When I grow up, maybe I'll be a star. Right now, I just want to be me!"

STRATEGY	EXAMPLES OF THE STRATEGY
Before reading, preview and determine the topic.	The story seems to be about a circus performer.

Name_____

STRATEGY	EXAMPLES OF THE STRATEGY
Then predict what will happen.	
Set a purpose for reading.	
During reading, change predictions if you need to.	
Write down what you visualize.	
After reading, summarize what you have read.	

With a partner, make a chart to help you remember the active reading strategies you have learned. Show your chart to your classmates. If you have room, hang it on a classroom wall where everyone can see it and refer to it.

FINDING THE GREEN STONE

Name_____

Read the clue on each barrel. Then write the words from the wheelbarrows on the correct barrels.

radiance

memory   realized

expectantly

concern   behavior

interest or worry
_____

shining brightness
_____

understood
_____

the way a person acts
_____

something remembered
_____

acting as if something will happen
_____

ACTIVITY CORNER

Write a silly sentence that includes four of the words on the wheelbarrows. Challenge a partner to write one, too. See whose sentence is sillier! (Just for fun: Try reading your sentence aloud five times without smiling!)

••• FINDING THE GREEN STONE •••

Name_____

A. Filling in a story frame can help you think about what a story means. Fill in this frame for "Finding the Green Stone."

   "Finding the Green Stone" takes place _____

_____.

The main characters are a brother and sister named

_____ and _____. They each have

_____, which they like very much.

The problem is that _____

_____. At first, Johnny feels _____

_____. Then, Katie helps him _____

_____. Other people, including _____

_____

_____ help, too. This makes Johnny feel

_____. The problem is solved then, because

_____. The green

stone is like a _____ feeling in Johnny's heart.

B. Now write a short summary of "Finding the Green Stone." _____

_____

_____

_____

Name_____

A. Read the paragraph below. Underline each compound sentence. Circle the word that joins the two simple sentences.

The green stone showed the kindness in each person's heart. Each sour word made the stone fade, and selfish deeds made it disappear completely. Johnny had a beautiful stone, but one morning the stone was gone. He missed it, and he went looking for it.

B. Join each pair of simple sentences with *and, but,* or *or* to form a compound sentence. Write the compound sentence on the line below.

Johnny tried to steal Katie's stone. It turned gray for him.

_____

He could forget about the stone. He could look for it.

_____

Write a compound sentence that tells two ideas about a green stone.

_____

_____

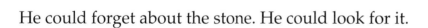

SUMMARIZING *the* **L**EARNING   Two simple sentences joined together form a

_____. A _____ is used

before the words *and, but,* and *or* when one of these words is used to join two sentences.

FINDING THE GREEN STONE

Name_____

Help Bloogle write his dictionary! Use context clues to decide what the words in dark print would mean if they were real words. Then explain to Bloogle why your meanings make sense.

1. Johnny goes into the **frammelhyser.** He looks at all the gifts and finally buys one for his sister.

I think a **frammelhyser** must be a

_____ because

_____

_____

_____ .

2. While Johnny is buying the gift, he notices a colorful, eye-catching **wrythromb.** It announces a writing contest to be held soon.

Bloogle, I think a **wrythromb**

must be a _____

because _____

_____

_____ .

Name_____

3. The **plymort** for the best entry is a new bicycle.

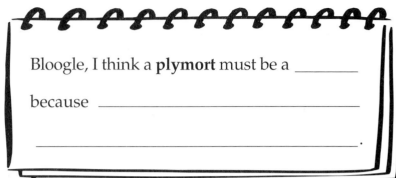

Bloogle, I think a **plymort** must be a _____

because _____

_____ .

4. "Katie needs a new bicycle," Johnny thinks. "Maybe I can **daffle** the bicycle and give it to her!"

I think **daffle** must mean _____

because _____

_____ .

5. "I'll write an exciting **valskur** about the time I lost my green stone!" Johnny decides.

Bloogle, I think a **valskur** must be a _____

_____ because _____

_____ .

It's your turn! Make up some sentences of your own. Replace one word in each sentence with a nonsense word. Challenge your partner to figure out what the nonsense words mean. Be sure to include context clues when you write your sentences.

• • • FINDING THE GREEN STONE • • •

Name_____

Be an author! First, look at the picture. Then write four
sentences about it, each with a different purpose.

Inform	Persuade

Entertain	Give Directions

Draw a picture of your own, and exchange pictures with a partner. Write
sentences about each other's pictures. Then trade again and try to determine
your partner's purpose for writing.

Name Kelsy McArthur

Use reading strategies to help you design a bulletin board about the story below. Read the story. Then complete each part of the bulletin board, using the strategy named.

THE CONTEST

No one, not even his parents, knew that Johnny had written a story and entered it in the writing contest. All the kids were excited about the contest, since the winner would receive a bicycle. Katie's birthday would be here soon, and Johnny was determined to win the bike for his sister. What a present that would be!

At last the day arrived when the winner would be announced. Johnny rushed through breakfast, so nervous he could hardly eat. He was just finishing his milk when the telephone rang.

"Hello," Johnny heard his mother say. "Oh, hello, Mrs. Banks . . . Of course you may. He's right here."

Johnny held his breath as he picked up the receiver.

Drawing Conclusions

The call must be about

_____.

The Contest

Understanding Cause and Effect

Johnny is nervous

because _____

_____.

Character Analysis

Johnny is the kind of

person who _____

_____.

Making Predictions

The next thing that will happen is

_____

_____.

Name_____

Find the right campaign button for each hat. Read the clue on each hat, and then write the word that fits the clue. The words you will need are on the buttons below.

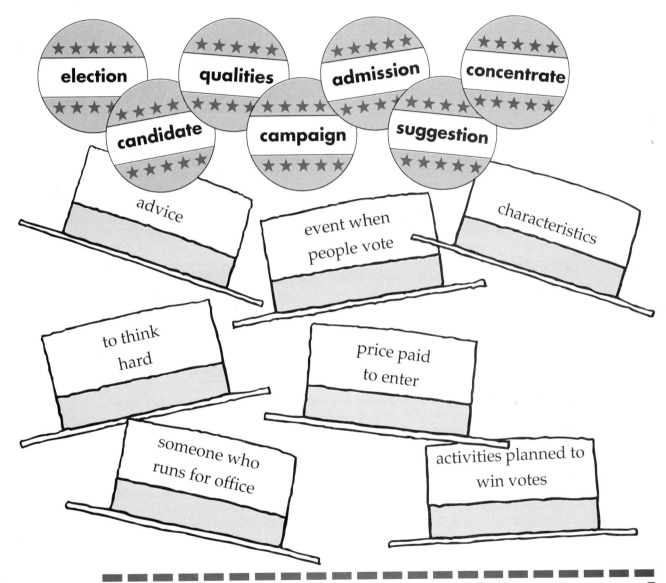

buttons: election, qualities, admission, concentrate, candidate, campaign, suggestion

hats:
- advice
- event when people vote
- characteristics
- to think hard
- price paid to enter
- someone who runs for office
- activities planned to win votes

Make a board game with a partner by drawing a long path of squares. On the squares, write words from the campaign buttons. Cut five strips of paper, and number them 1 to 5. Turn the numbered strips face down and draw one. Move your game marker that number of squares. Give a synonym for the word you land on, or use it in a sentence.

Name_____

A. One way to summarize a story is to complete a story frame. Finish the story frame below to summarize "Class President."

"Class President" takes place _____

_____. _____ is a character who

_____.

A problem occurs when _____

_____. After that, _____

_____. Next, _____

_____. The problem

is solved when _____.

The story ends when _____

_____.

B. Write a brief summary statement about the story.

_____

_____

_____

• • • CLASS PRESIDENT • • •

Name_____

Know your leaders! Write the answer for each riddle.
The words you will need are on the banner.

Vice-President Mayor Congress Governor State Legislator

I become the leader if the President can't serve. Who am I?
_____

I help make the laws for the United States. Where do I serve?
_____

I am the leader of my town. Who am I?
_____

I am the head of my state's government. Who am I?
_____

I help make the laws for my state. Who am I?
_____

With your classmates, make a Government Chart. Find out the names of the leaders of your state and local governments. On the chart, write their names and their offices.

••• CLASS PRESIDENT •••

Name_____

A. Read the paragraph below. Underline the subject of each sentence once. Underline each predicate twice.

Our class held an election last Wednesday. All of the candidates made brief speeches. Ravi's speech was excellent. Ravi is a promising candidate.

B. Add a subject or a predicate to each sentence part to make a complete sentence. Write your complete sentence on the line below the sentence part.

my classmates

_____

clapped loudly for Elena's speech

_____

the cheering students

_____

voted for Sara

_____

Write a sentence or two about an election campaign. Make sure each sentence has a subject and a predicate.

_____

SUMMARIZING the LEARNING The two parts of a sentence are the _____ and the

_____. The _____ tells who or what the sentence is

about. The _____ tells what the subject is or does.

Name_____

Julio is writing a report. Help the librarian answer his questions about where to find the information he needs.

Which volume of the encyclopedia will tell me what manatees eat?

_____

I need to know whether the Gulf of Mexico is closer to the Atlantic Ocean or the Pacific Ocean. Should I look at the globe or in the encyclopedia?

_____

Where should I look to find out how far it is from Miami, Florida, to Atlanta, Georgia?

_____

Which encyclopedia volume will tell me about animals that live in the Amazon River?

_____

ACTIVITY CORNER

Choose a topic that interests both you and a partner. Use an encyclopedia, an atlas, and a globe to find out at least five facts about the topic. Share what you learn with your classmates.

••• CLASS PRESIDENT •••

Name_____

Kim is preparing a report about presidential campaigns. Read the following paragraph. Then help Kim complete her chart.

CAMPAIGN SOUVENIRS

Buttons, pins, posters, banners—you *see* them everywhere during presidential campaigns. As early as 1789 Americans were sewing *Long Live the President* buttons on their clothing to celebrate George Washington's presidency. Many people collect campaign souvenirs as a hobby, and some of the objects they have found might surprise you. For example, a cast-iron doorstop in the shape of a frog boosted Andrew Jackson's campaign in 1828. On the back of the frog were the words "I croak for the Jackson wagon." Umbrellas with the candidate's name printed on them were popular campaign items in the late 1800s.

Question-Answer Relationship				
Question	Right There	Think and Search	On My Own	Answer
When did Americans begin wearing campaign buttons?				
What are some examples of unusual campaign souvenirs?				
Why do people like collecting political souvenirs?				

20   **Analyzing Details**

Practice Book ■ **EMERALD FOREST**

HBJ material copyrighted under notice appearing earlier in this work.

Name_____

Use what you know about Julio to predict what he will say in each of the situations below. Write Julio's words, and then explain your prediction.

 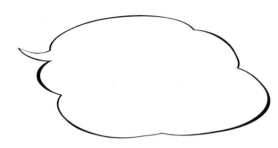

One of Julio's classmates cries when he skins his knee playing soccer.

How do you know? _____

 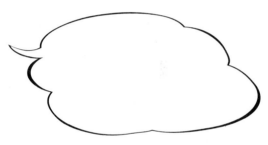

A new student joins Julio's class. Nobody chooses him to play soccer at recess.

How do you know? _____

 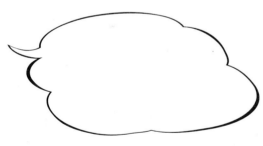

Julio needs to figure out how to make brownies.

How do you know? _____

What do you think will happen when the class votes for class president? With a partner, write another chapter for the story. Tell who you think will win. Compare your chapter with the ones your classmates write.

Name_____

Create some clues! Read each mystery word and its meaning. Then write a sentence using the word. Try to write your sentence so that another reader would be able to figure out what the mystery word means.

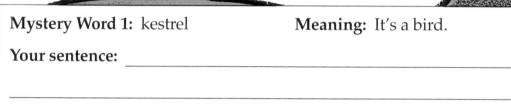

Mystery Word 1: kestrel   **Meaning:** It's a bird.

Your sentence: _____

_____

Mystery Word 2: potentate   **Meaning:** It's a king.

Your sentence: _____

_____

Mystery Word 3: prevail   **Meaning:** It means to win.

Your sentence: _____

_____

Mystery Word 4: chapeau   **Meaning:** It's a hat.

Your sentence: _____

_____

ACTIVITY CORNER

Search the dictionary for some unusual words. Write a sentence that uses each word and includes context clues. Challenge your partner to figure out what the mystery words mean!

Name_____

Make your way to the finish line of this bicycle race.
Write the answer to each question, using the words
on the bicycles.

[words on the bicycles: muscles, overtook, pedal, wrinkles, cyclists, official, intention]

RENERO

1. What do you push with your foot to make a bike go? _____

2. What is another word for a plan? _____

3. What are persons who ride bikes called? _____

4. What do you call small folds on skin? _____

5. What means "passed by"? _____

6. What tissues make your body parts move? _____

7. What is another word for "approved by authorities"? _____

FINISH

Have a "bicycle race" with a group of classmates. On a sheet of paper, mark off nine
squares. Label the first square "S" for "Start" and the last one "F" for "Finish." Have
another student read aloud one of the words on the bicycles. If you can tell what the
word means, move from "Start" to the next square. Keep going until you miss or until
you reach "Finish." See who can go the farthest!

··· SUPERGRANDPA ···

Name_____

A. Complete this story map to summarize "Supergrandpa."

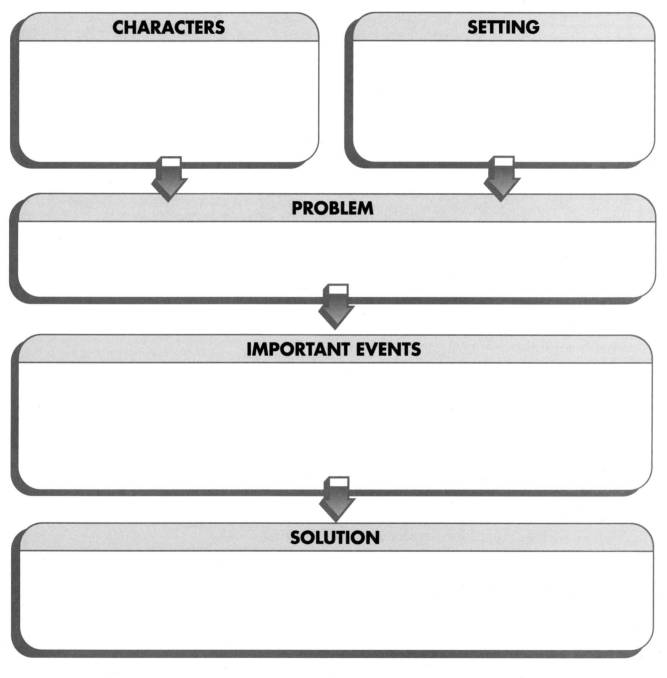

CHARACTERS

SETTING

PROBLEM

IMPORTANT EVENTS

SOLUTION

B. Summarize the story in one or two sentences. _____

_____

_____

••• SUPERGRANDPA •••

Name_____

A. Read the paragraph below. Circle each simple subject.
Underline any compound subjects you find.

Hulda Crooks broke a world record in 1987. This 91-
year-old climber wanted to be the oldest woman to
climb Mount Fuji in Japan. The record holder at that
time was a 90-year-old Japanese woman.

Crooks and her team stood triumphantly on the
summit three days after starting up the mountain.

B. Complete the sentences, using any subject that
makes sense.

_____ helps build strong muscles.

_____ are popular sports in the United States.

Write about a contest you have seen or have taken part in.
Circle your complete subjects.

_____

_____

• •

SUMMARIZING
the **L**EARNING The _____ contains *all* the words that tell

who or what a sentence is about. The _____ is the main word

or words that tell exactly who or what the sentence is about. When two subjects share

the same predicate and are joined by *and,* they form a _____ .

Name_____

A. Lara is writing a report about bicycle racing. Help her decide where to find the information she needs. Choose from the book parts listed on the pages.

title page	table of contents
copyright page	index

I need to find out when this book was published.

Look on the

_____.

Who is the author of this book?

Try looking on the

_____.

I'd like to find out which pages mention the Tour de France.

I would look in the

_____.

I remember reading about bicycle safety in this book. What was the title of that chapter?

You can find out in the

_____.

Name_____

B. Help! The pieces of this book are all mixed up! Help the editor decide where each piece of information belongs. Choose from the book parts listed on page 26.

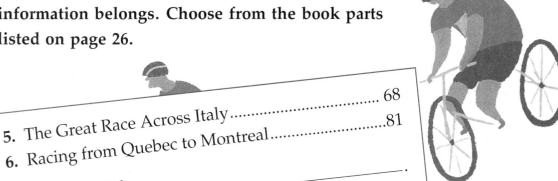

5. The Great Race Across Italy.............................. 68
6. Racing from Quebec to Montreal.........................81

This is part of the _____.

Great Bicycle Races of the World   This belongs on the
by Martin L. Overton

_____.

Handlebars, types, 8, 11   Put this information in the
Helmets, use of, 4, 18, 31

_____.

Copyright 1992   This should go on the
by Martin L. Overton

_____.

Working with a group, compare the tables of contents in different books and magazines. Try to find some that use different colors and kinds of print. What do you think makes a good table of contents? Share your ideas with some classmates.

Name_____

Read the travel journal entry. Decide which strategy the detective could use to figure out the meaning of each underlined word. Then complete the sentences below by writing *context clues, structural clues,* or *picture clues.*

> Here I am in Sweden! What a beautiful country this is, with its snow-topped mountains and picturesque lakes. Yesterday I tried the famous Swedish smorgasbord. HERRING There were so many hot and cold foods on the table that I hardly knew what to put on my plate first! Everything was so delicious that I ate avidly.

Hmmmm. Since the writer says the country is beautiful, *picturesque* must mean "pretty." I used _____ to figure this out.

This is easy! The _____ tell me that a herring is a kind of fish. *Smorgasbord* must be an assortment of hot and cold foods. I figured this out by using _____ .

The suffix *-ly* means "in a certain way." Since the writer thought the food was delicious, *avidly* must mean "eagerly" or perhaps "quickly." I know this from both _____ and _____ .

With a partner, read about Sweden in an encyclopedia or another reference book. When you find an unfamiliar word, talk about the strategies you can use to figure out the word's meaning. Make a list of the words you learn, and share them with your classmates.

Name_____

What's your prediction? Read each paragraph.
Then write what you think will happen next.
Be sure to explain your answer.

Supergrandpa is making his
lunch. He discovers he's out of fruit.
The nearest store is two miles away,
and he doesn't have a car.

What Supergrandpa will do:
_____
_____

Why I think so: _____
_____
_____

Supergrandpa's neighbor tells him
that older people should not exercise
very much.

What Supergrandpa will say:
_____
_____

Why I think so: _____
_____
_____

Supergrandpa reads in the
newspaper that next year, riders of all
ages will be allowed to enter the Tour
of Sweden.

What Supergrandpa will do:
_____
_____

Why I think so: _____
_____
_____

SUPERGRANDPA

Name_____

Choose one of the activities below. Work by yourself or with a classmate to do the activity.

ACTIVITY 1

Read a book, a story, or an article about bicycle races. Use context clues to help you figure out the meanings of unfamiliar words. Then make your own mini-dictionary of the words and their definitions. Share your dictionary with your classmates.

ACTIVITY 2

Write a story about an older person who can do something unusual. (Your story does not have to be true.) Be sure to put in context clues to help your readers figure out words they may not know. Bind your finished copy, and let your classmates read it.

ACTIVITY 3

Design a poster to remind readers to use context clues. Make your poster colorful and eye-catching. When it's finished, hang it in the classroom where everyone can see it.

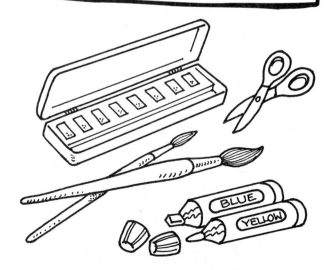

• • • CHARLOTTE'S WEB • • •

Name _____

Read each pair of sentences. The second sentence in each pair includes a word that means the same as the underlined word or phrase. Draw a line around the word.

1. Each drop of water <u>sparkled</u> in the tall grass.
The pond glistened in the early morning sun.

2. After her <u>hard work</u> baling the hay, Kaila went swimming.
Her exertions had made her tired and hot.

3. When Rick opened the barn door, he expected to see the <u>usual</u> sights.
The day had started out as ordinary as any other day.

4. Everyone noticed Nathan's <u>strange habit</u> of talking to his tractor.
Nathan himself couldn't explain this idiosyncrasy.

5. No one knows <u>what is bound to happen</u> to the runaway horse.
Its destiny is surely not to pull a plow.

6. The wings of a butterfly are <u>thin and easily torn</u>.
Many insects have extremely delicate wings.

Practice Book ▪ EMERALD FOREST   **Vocabulary**   **31**

• • • CHARLOTTE'S WEB • • •

Name _____

A. One way to summarize a story is to complete a chain of events showing what happens. The chain of events has been started below. Finish it by completing the sentences.

1. Charlotte wants to help Wilbur.

2. She weaves "SOME PIG" into her web.

3. Lurvy sees this and tells Mr. Zuckerman.

6. The news

5. Then Mr. Zuckerman

4. Mr. Zuckerman

7. Charlotte worries that

8. So she

9. The animals suggest

11. At the end,

10. Templeton agrees to

B. Write a brief summary statement about the story, using your chain of events.

_____

_____

• • • CHARLOTTE'S WEB • • •

Name _____

Choose the boldface homophone that correctly completes the
sentence. Write it on the line. Then write a sentence using the
other boldface homophone.

1. Fern _____ that her uncle and Lurvy would take
good care of Wilbur.
knows   **nose**

_____

2. Homer Zuckerman and Lurvy do _____ best to
take care of the pig.
there   **their**

_____

3. The animals tell Wilbur that he might be the _____
course at the Christmas dinner.
mane   **main**

_____

4. The first message Charlotte weaves is "_____ pig!"
some   **sum**

_____

5. When Lurvy first sees the web, he feels _____.
week   **weak**

_____

6. Mr. Zuckerman tells his wife that a sign has occurred right

_____ on earth.
here   **hear**

_____

CHARLOTTE'S WEB

Name_____

A. Underline the complete predicate in each sentence below. Then circle any compound predicates.

Spiders have eight legs and two main body sections.

Spiders spin silk and use the silk to make webs. Some spiders

can make poison. Only a few spiders are dangerous to humans.

B. Use a simple predicate from the box to complete each sentence. Then underline each complete predicate.

eat
live
dig

Trap-door spiders _____ a burrow in which they live

and which they use to help them capture food. Many tarantulas,

the world's largest spiders, _____ in the southwestern

United States. Fisher spiders _____ water insects,

tadpoles, and small fish.

Write a sentence about a spider. Underline the complete predicate.

_____

SUMMARIZING *the* **L**EARNING   A complete predicate is made up of all the words in a sentence

that describe what a subject _____ or _____. To locate the

_____ of a sentence, find the key word in the complete

predicate. When you use the word _____ to combine two sentences with

the same subject, you are making a _____.

HBJ material copyrighted under notice appearing earlier in this work.

Name_____

Ed, the magazine editor, is frantic! Authors have sent him
several different kinds of fiction, and he needs your help
to sort their work. On the note clipped to each page, write
fantasy, realistic fiction, or *play.*

Amigo

As soon as Steve arrived at his grandparents' farm, he
headed straight for the horse barn to see his friend, Amigo.
"Hello, old fellow," he said quietly. Amigo lifted his head and
whinnied softly. Soon he was nuzzling Steve's shirt pocket,
looking for the special treat he was sure to find there.

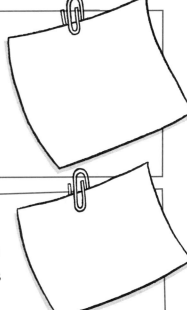

Molly's Lamb

SETTING: The yard of a farm house

DAD   *(Entering from stage left):* Molly, come here – and
        hurry! I have something to show you.

MOLLY *(Standing up quickly):* Has Sadie had her lamb?

Storm at Thunder Ranch

It was sunny only a few minutes ago, but now dark clouds hid the
sun. Milkshake, the oldest cow, lifted her head and sniffed. "Rain's
coming!" she mooed. "Everybody into the barn!"

Work with a group to list the fiction books and stories you have read
recently. Beside each title, write *fantasy, realistic fiction, play,* or another label
to identify the type of fiction.

Name _____

A. Read the following article. Then write the important parts and a summary statement in the chart.

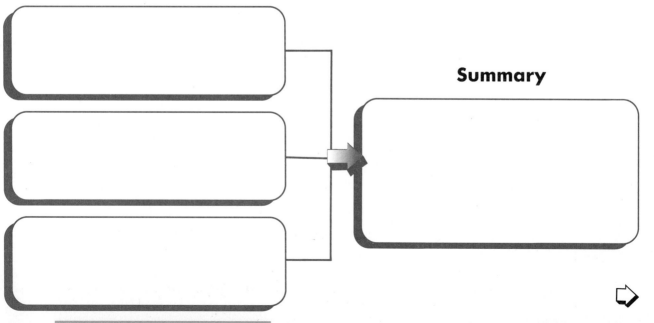

Spiders: Their Webs and Their Habits

Most people do not realize how much a spider depends on its ability to spin webs. Although some spiders don't need webs all the time, others are helpless without them. When a baby spider comes out of its egg, the first thing it does is spin a dragline. This is two or more large threads that are so closely joined that they seem to be a single strand. This dragline strings behind the spider for its entire life, unless it is accidentally broken.

The dragline can be compared to the rope of a mountain climber. Like the mountain climber's rope, it allows the spider to drop from a web and still be safe. Attached to its dragline, a spider can hide in a plant or suspend itself in midair and then climb back to its original position.

Important Parts

Summary

Name _____

B. Read the following article. Then complete the chart.

Hunters

Some spiders hunt for prey in the daytime. Others hunt at night. One of the most interesting of the night-hunting spiders is the bolas spider. This spider is found in many parts of the United States, in Africa, and in Australia. Bolas spiders do not spin webs to trap prey, nor do they pounce on their victims. Instead, they throw a lasso.

To make these lassos, bolas spiders first spin a silk thread. Then they place a tiny ball of sticky silk on the end of the thread. Then the bolas spider uses this weapon to "rope" flying insects. Stopped in midair, the insect can rarely escape, since the silky thread of the spider can stretch an additional fifth of its length before breaking.

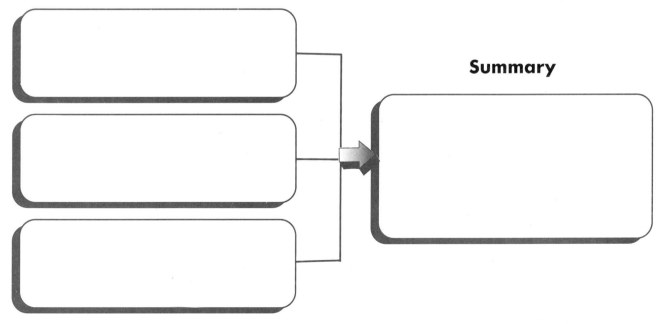

Important Parts

Summary

Name_____

Find the word on the pet dish that answers each clue. Then write the word on the paw print next to the clue.

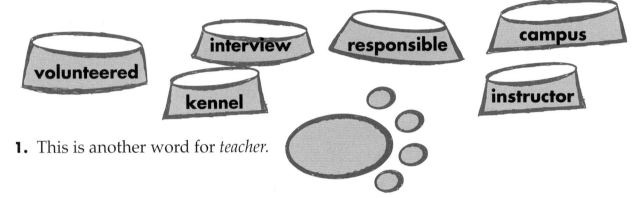

1. This is another word for *teacher*.

2. If you ask a person questions to get information, you are

conducting an _____ .

3. This word is a synonym for *dependable* and *reliable*.

4. Dogs are kept in this.

5. What do you call the grounds and buildings of a school?

6. If you offered to do something, you _____ .

Play "What's My Word?" with a group of five classmates. Write each word from the pet dishes on a separate slip of paper. Ask someone not in your group to tape a word on the back of each player. Your job is to figure out which word is taped to your own back by asking the other players questions that can be answered with *yes* or *no*.

••• A GUIDE DOG PUPPY GROWS UP •••

Name_____

A. One way to summarize a nonfiction selection is to fill in a K-W-L chart. Complete the chart below.

K	W	L
What I Know	What I Want to Know	What I Learned

B. Use the information in your chart to write a brief summary statement about what you learned.

_____

_____

_____

_____

HBJ material copyrighted under notice appearing earlier in this work.

Name_____

On the lines, write words that appeal to the senses and that describe the object in the picture. Then write a sentence about the object, using some of the words you have listed.

Sight: _____   Taste: _____

Hearing: _____   Touch: _____

Smell: _____

Your sentence: _____

Sight: _____   Taste: _____

Hearing: _____   Touch: _____

Smell: _____

Your sentence: _____

Sight: _____   Taste: _____

Hearing: _____   Touch: _____

Smell: _____   _____

Your sentence: _____

_____

ACTIVITY CORNER

Work with a group to make a chart of words you find in your reading that appeal to the senses. Post your chart in the classroom, and add to it as you read.

Name_____

A. Read the paragraph below. Circle all the common nouns and underline all the proper nouns.

The dog who worked the longest time was a retriever

named Cindy-Cleo, according to *The Guinness Book of World Records.*

She was owned by Aaron Barr of Tel Aviv, Israel, and she worked

for 14 years and 8 months!

B. Write a noun on each line to create the beginning of a story.

My _____ is the most helpful and friendly animal
      (type of animal)

in the world! She was born in _____, where she learned to help
                                 (place name)

people look for _____. Her real name is _____,
                    (thing)   (name)

but I call her _____.
                  (nickname)

Write a sentence or two about something you and an animal friend might do together. Use at least one common noun and one proper noun.

_____

SUMMARIZING
the **L**EARNING   A noun that names any person, place, or thing is called a

_____. A noun that names a _____ person, place,

or thing is called a _____. In proper nouns that contain more than

one word, each important word begins with a _____.

••• A GUIDE DOG PUPPY GROWS UP •••

Name_____

A. Read each paragraph. On each notepad, write a sentence that states the main idea of the paragraph. Underline any details in the paragraph that do not support the main idea.

Puppy raisers must take their job seriously. Of course, they must treat the puppy well, as any family pet should be treated, and they should play with it often. Some puppy trainers raise many puppies over the years. They must also teach the puppy how to behave in public.

If you visited the campus of Guide Dogs for the Blind, you would find a large kennel where more than 300 dogs live. You would also find a building where people live while they are learning how to work with their dogs. Another building is for offices. Golden retrievers make good Guide Dogs.

Guide Dogs help their owners cross busy streets. Do not pet a Guide Dog without the owner's permission. They pick up dropped objects. They can even guide their owners up and down stairs. The dogs' skills make life easier for their owners.

Name_____

B. Finish this paragraph about Guide Dogs. Add at least two details to support the main idea.

A Guide Dog is a hard-working animal.

C. Now, write a paragraph of your own. Be sure all the details support the main idea.

Write a "team paragraph" with a group of classmates. First, choose a main idea. Then, each group member should contribute a sentence that adds a detail. Work together to revise the paragraph so that it flows smoothly.

••• A Guide Dog Puppy Grows Up •••

Name_____

A. Ling is working with the computerized card catalog in his school's library. Use the information on the computer screen to help him answer his questions.

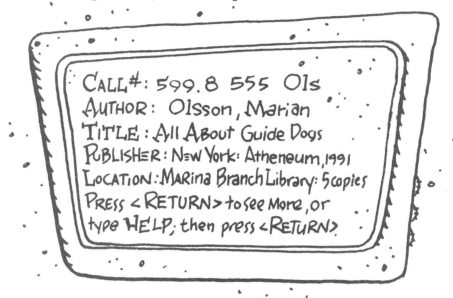

CALL#: 599.8 555 Ols
AUTHOR: Olsson, Marian
TITLE: All About Guide Dogs
PUBLISHER: New York: Atheneum, 1991
LOCATION: Marina Branch Library: 5 copies
PRESS <RETURN> to see More, or
type HELP; then press <RETURN>

Who is the author of this book?

_____

What is the name of the publisher?

_____

How many copies does the branch library have?

_____

What should I do to find more books about Guide Dogs?

_____

What should I do to get help from the computer?

_____

••• A GUIDE DOG PUPPY GROWS UP •••

Name_____

B. Karla is a new student who has never used a card catalog.
Write what you would say to her to explain how to use it.

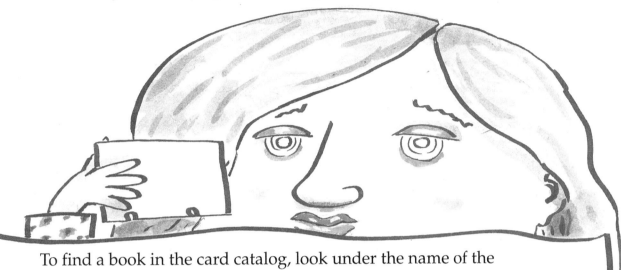

To find a book in the card catalog, look under the name of the

_____ or under the _____ or the _____.

The cards are in _____ order. When you find the right card,

look at the numbers and letters on the _____ side of the card.

For fiction books, the letters on the card are the first few letters of the

_____. You will find the book in the fiction section,

arranged in _____ order under the author's name. For

nonfiction books, look at the _____ on the card. These tell

you what section the book is in. If you need help, _____.

Work with a group to write a short play about how to use the card catalog in
your school library. After you have practiced, present the play to your classmates
or to a group of younger students.

HBJ material copyrighted under notice appearing earlier in this work.

Name _____

A. Read each sentence below. Then choose the word in parentheses that fits the meaning of the sentence and write it on the line.

1. Nancy hurried through the _____ of trees and bushes, hoping to reach the cabin soon. (thicket, bank)

2. Suddenly, she heard a crash followed by

   a sharp cry of pain and _____. (laughter, fury)

3. The cries increased in _____ as Nancy moved deeper into the woods. (intensity, worth)

4. After _____ the underbrush, she found a dog caught in the branches of a fallen tree. (probing, avoiding)

5. She leaned over the fearful, _____ creature. (confident, cowering)

6. The poor animal seemed _____ of the human. (suspicious, weary)

7. Nancy _____ hurting the dog by lifting the branches carefully. (researched, avoided)

8. Showing amazing _____, the dog limped behind her to the cabin. (endurance, weakness)

B. On a separate sheet of paper, write sentences of your own. Use the words *intensity, endurance, suspicious,* and *fury*.

Name _____

A. One way to summarize a story is to complete a cause-and-effect chain. Finish the chain below by writing endings to the sentences in the boxes.

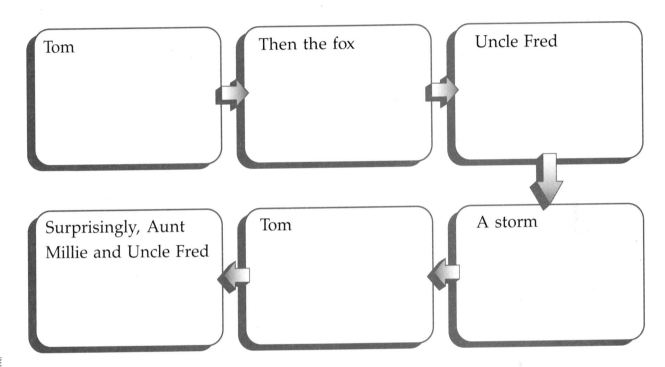

Tom

Then the fox

Uncle Fred

A storm

Tom

Surprisingly, Aunt Millie and Uncle Fred

B. Use the information in your cause-and-effect chain to write a brief summary statement about the story.

_____

_____

_____

_____

Name _____

A. Read each sentence below and think about the underlined simile or metaphor. In the space provided, explain in your own words what each sentence from the story means.

1. I just stood with the sun beating down on my head <u>like a</u>

<u>fist</u> . . . _____

_____

2. <u>Like a charging bull</u>, he entered the thicket. . . . _____

_____

3. "Are you all right? Your face is <u>beet red</u>." _____

_____

4. "Just <u>like a baby lamb</u>," she said. _____

_____

5. . . . the sky to the west had gotten <u>black as ink</u>. _____

_____

B. Write a simile or a metaphor of your own to describe the baby fox. It may describe the fox at any time—before it is captured, while it is trapped, or after Tom sets it free.

_____

_____

_____

Name_____

A. **Read the paragraph below, and circle every proper noun.**

During the summer, Olivia went to visit

Uncle Cerney. She arrived on a Monday in late June.

The entire neighborhood, including Mr. Westmoreland

and Dr. Jaffe, went to Kansas City on Independence Day

for a big picnic.

B. **Rewrite each sentence, capitalizing the proper nouns.**

1. Uncle cerney lived near a city named eudora.

_____

2. He and his son bradley took their dogs, riley and jake, for a walk beside pomona lake.

_____

_____

3. There was a storm on wednesday when they left.

_____

Write a sentence with a common noun and a proper noun.

_____

•••

SUMMARIZING
the **L**EARNING   A noun that names a particular holiday, day of the week, or

month is a _____. The first letter of each important word in a

proper noun should be _____.

••• THE MIDNIGHT FOX •••

Name_____

A. Read the following story beginning. Then fill in your answers to the questions on the next page.

ESCAPE!

Karen bent into the cold wind and scuffed her boots through the snow. The cloud-darkened sky did nothing to lighten her mood.

"Even the weather is against me," she thought gloomily. Karen was convinced that this was the worst day of her life. Today the girls' chorus at her school had elected officers. Karen had wanted so much to be president! "I love chorus," she had told her best friend, Jenny. "It's the best part of the whole day! I'll really work hard if I'm elected."

But Karen hadn't won. And who had beaten her? Jenny! Karen hadn't been able to keep the tears from her eyes when the votes were counted: Jenny 18, Karen 17.

"How could she run against me?" Karen stormed. "She knew how much I wanted to be president, and she doesn't even like chorus very much. How could she do this to me?"

After the election, the day had dragged on until finally the last bell had rung. Still feeling sorry for herself, Karen was plodding home. Across the street from her house, she paused and stared in surprise. Jenny's back gate hung wide open, swinging back and forth in the wind.

"Oh, no!" Karen moaned. "The wind must have blown the gate open. Now Kona is gone!" Kona was Jenny's cocker spaniel. Ever since Jenny's parents had divorced, Jenny had grown more and more devoted to the little dog.

The sight of the open gate drove everything else from Karen's mind. She rushed up onto the porch to ring the doorbell. "We've got to find him!" she thought frantically.

••• THE MIDNIGHT FOX •••

Name_____

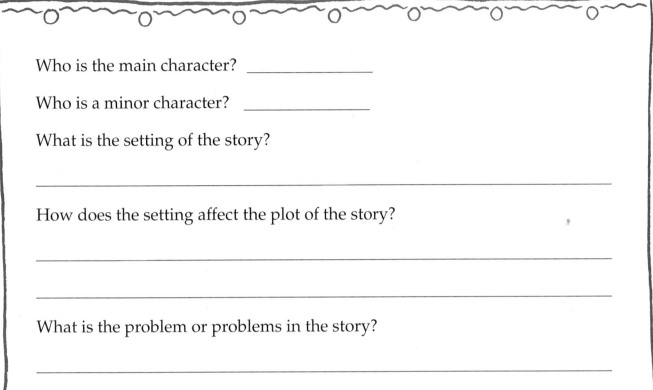

Who is the main character? _____

Who is a minor character? _____

What is the setting of the story?

_____

How does the setting affect the plot of the story?

_____

_____

What is the problem or problems in the story?

_____

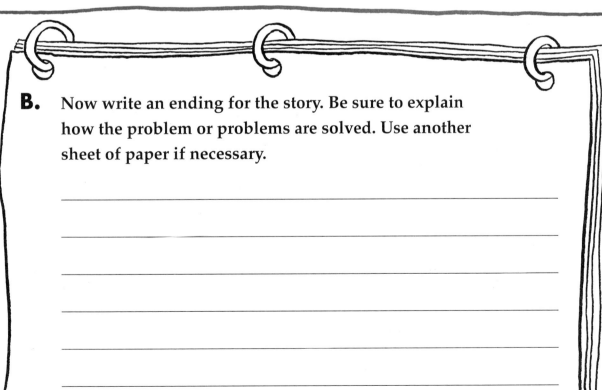

B. Now write an ending for the story. Be sure to explain how the problem or problems are solved. Use another sheet of paper if necessary.

_____

_____

_____

_____

_____

• • • THE MIDNIGHT FOX • • •

Name _____

A. The sentences below are out of order. Arrange each group of
sentences into a paragraph, writing the topic sentence first and
then writing the sentences that give supporting details.

He was following a new scent. He entered the thicket and
went right to the foxes' den. He went through the forest, nose
to the ground. Happ seemed to be on the foxes' trail.

_____

_____

_____

He held the tree very tightly before he began to inch down
the trunk. Tom found it very scary to climb down the tree during
the storm. It took a long time to get enough courage just to
move. He never even looked down until he touched the grass.

_____

_____

_____

B. Choose one of the following topic sentences. Write three
supporting details to go with it.

The baby fox was obviously very frightened.
The mother fox was determined to help her baby.

_____

_____

52   *Main Idea and Details*   Practice Book ■ **EMERALD FOREST**

HBJ material copyrighted under notice appearing earlier in this work.

• • • DREAM WOLF • • •

Name _____

Look at each picture. Choose a word or words from the box to complete each caption.

> kinship   roams   wounded   twilight   shelter

1. A young wolf, _____ by a hunter, is separated from the pack.

2. Feelings of _____ among members of a pack are strong.

3. All day until _____ , the rest of the pack _____ the hills.

4. The pack stops to _____ in a cave.

HBJ material copyrighted under notice appearing earlier in this work.

Name _____

A. One way to summarize a story is to record key story
elements in a sequence chain. Complete the sequence
chain below by writing story events in the boxes.

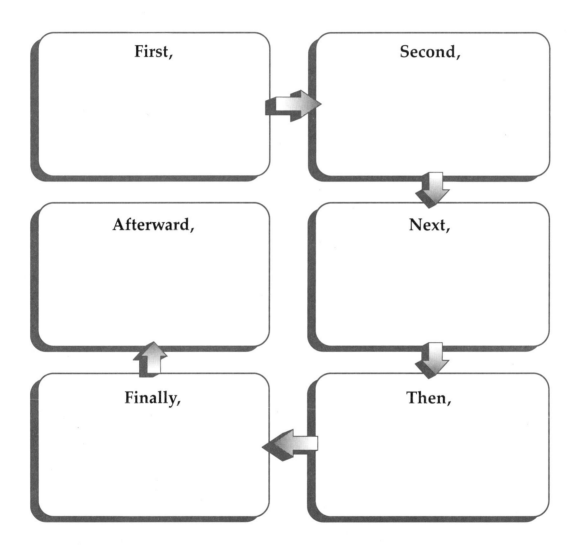

First,

Second,

Afterward,

Next,

Finally,

Then,

B. Use the information in your sequence chain to write a
brief summary statement.

_____

_____

_____

Name _____

A. Read each example of personification below. Rewrite each
sentence so that its meaning is the same, but without using
personification.

1. The sun played a game of hide-and-seek, using the

   clouds as a cover. _____

2. The old tree moaned with pain in the cold wind. _____

   _____

3. The blanket gave out a dusty cough as it was shaken open. _____

   _____

4. The wood refused to cooperate when Tiblo tried to light the

   campfire. _____

B. Rewrite each sentence so that its meaning is the same, but use
personification to make it more interesting.

1. It was sunny out. _____

2. There was a small cave among the rocks. _____

   _____

3. The sun was setting behind the hills. _____

   _____

4. The children's campfire began to go out. _____

   _____

••• DREAM WOLF •••

Name_____

A. Read the paragraph below. Look carefully at the *underlined* words.

    The <u>wolf</u> is a very good <u>hunter</u>. It often hunts large hoofed <u>animals</u>, such as <u>deer</u>. Most wolves live in <u>groups</u> called packs. Wolves once lived in many places in this <u>country</u>, but <u>men</u> have hunted them nearly to extinction. Today wolves are mostly found in Alaska, Minnesota, and Canada.

B. If a singular noun is shown below, make it plural. If a plural noun is shown, make it singular.

Singular	Plural	Singular	Plural
wolf	→ _____	group	→ _____
_____	→ hunters	pack	→ _____
_____	→ animals	country	→ _____
_____	→ deer	→	men

Write one or two sentences about wolves. Use at least one singular noun and one plural noun from your list above.

_____

_____

SUMMARIZING *the* **L**EARNING Words that name one person, one place, or one thing are called _____. Words that name more than one person, place, or thing are called _____. Add _____ to make most singular nouns plural.

• • • DREAM WOLF • • • •

Name _____

Read the story below, and then read what one student thought as she read it. Think about what strategy or strategies she used to decode the underlined words. Choose one or more strategies from this list: *base word, prefix, suffix, suffix changes how the word is used,* and *dictionary.* Write your choices in each thought balloon.

At Camp WonderDaze, Jacy decided to go hiking by himself. He knew that he shouldn't go off as a solo <u>hiker</u> in the wilderness. Even so, he left camp without telling anyone.

Soon, Jacy realized that he was lost. He <u>thoroughly</u> checked every item in his backpack for a compass or a map, but he had <u>disregarded</u> his counselor's advice and had left without them.

When Jacy looked up, a wolf jumped into his path. Suddenly it was <u>impossible</u> for Jacy to move. As he stared at the wolf, he heard someone call his <u>name</u>, and the wolf bounded into the forest.

> Jacy is called a hiker. I know that the suffix *-er* means "one who." Jacy is one who hikes.
> _____

> The suffix *-ly* tells *how* Jacy checks every item in his backpack, so *thoroughly* must mean "carefully."
> _____
> _____

> I know that the prefix *dis-* means "not" or "opposite of," but I don't know what *regard* means. So, I'll look it up in the dictionary.
> _____
> _____

> If something is possible, I can do it. The prefix *im-* means "not," so *impossible* means "not able to do."
> _____

Name _____

A. Read each sentence below. On the line, write *first person* or *third person* to identify the point of view.

1. Tiblo and his little sister went berry-picking with the women

of the tribe. _____

2. Tanksi was a joy to her family and to the tribe. _____

3. I wanted to help the children. They were lost. _____

4. The children fell asleep in the cave. _____

5. The wolf led us to the camp. _____

B. Read each sentence below. Rewrite each one in the requested point of view.

1. As I walked toward the camp, I saw the people of our tribe coming toward me and smiling.

Third person: _____

_____

2. When they were children, Tiblo and Tanksi were very adventurous.

First person: _____

_____

Name _____

A. Read each sentence below. Draw a line under the word or words following the sentence that mean the same as the word in dark print.

1. At one time, wild animals were **prey** for hunters who killed them for food.

   dangerous   extinct animals   hunted animals   fearful

2. Now, some wild animals are **endangered** more by the growth of cities than by hunters' rifles.

   frightened   put in danger   captured   tamed

3. Herds of elephants, antelope, and zebras once **occupied** large parts of Africa.

   lived in   destroyed   discovered   ignored

4. Little by little, people built towns and cities in areas that were once **wilderness.**

   battlefields   parklands   flooded   unsettled land

5. Governments in Africa are now setting aside land to make sure that wild animals **survive.**

   suffer   remain in existence   don't hurt people

B. Use the words *endangered, occupied,* and *wilderness* in sentences of your own.

1. _____

2. _____

3. _____

Name _____

A. One way to summarize a nonfiction selection is to complete a
K-W-L chart. Complete the chart below.

K *What I Know*	W *What I Want to Know*	L *What I Learned*

B. Use information from your chart to write a brief summary
statement about the selection.

_____

_____

••• RUNNING WITH THE PACK •••

Name_____

A. Read the paragraph below. Circle the singular possessive nouns. Underline the plural possessive nouns.

    The pups' mother lay sleeping on the floor of the cave. The pups played around her. They nipped each other and crawled over their mother's calm body. The wolf's growl told the pups to settle down. After the pups lay down, the young animals' eyes began to close. Soon, they were sound asleep.

B. Write the possessive form of each underlined noun on the lines below.

the howling of the <u>coyotes</u>	the trunks of the <u>elephants</u>
the _____ howling	the _____ trunks
the tail of the <u>gopher</u>	the toys of the <u>children</u>
the _____ tail	the _____ toys

Use one of the possessive noun phrases above to write a complete sentence on the line below.

_____

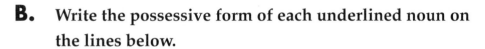

SUMMARIZING *the* **L**EARNING   A noun that shows ownership is formed by adding

_____ to the end of the word. Most plural nouns that show

ownership are formed by adding _____ to the end of the word.

Name_____

Study the dictionary entry below. Then write your answers on
the computer screens.

> **wolf** [wo͝olf] *n., pl.* **wolves** [wo͞olvz] **1** *n.* Any of a group of wild animals
> related to the dog. Wolves usually hunt in packs and prey on other animals.
> **2** *n.* Any ravenous, greedy, or cruel person or thing. **3** *v.* To eat in a greedy
> manner; gulp down; devour. — **cry wolf** To give a false alarm. —**keep the wolf
> from the door** To keep from being hungry or needy. —**wolf'ish** *adj.*

How many definitions are given for the word *wolf*?

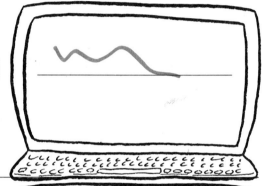

What does *wolf* mean when used as a verb?

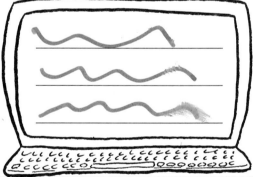

What part of speech is the word *wolfish*?

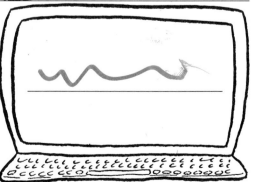

Name_____

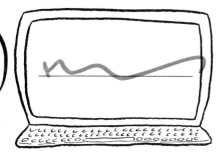

Which meaning of the word *wolf* is this: They feared they would be letting a wolf into the house if they opened the door to a stranger.

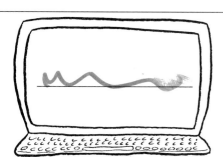

What is the plural of *wolf*?

What are you doing if you are " just crying wolf"?

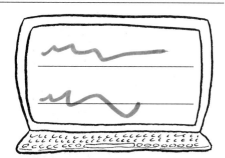

What does *keep the wolf from the door* mean?

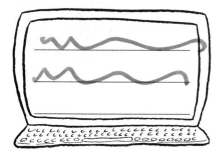

ACTIVITY CORNER

With a group of classmates, find several interesting words that you don't know. Look them up, and then write the meanings in your own words. You may want to draw pictures to help show the meanings.

••• RUNNING WITH THE PACK •••

Name _____

A. Read each main idea below. Write three supporting details that could be included with it in a paragraph.

1. Pat and a small group of friends went camping last weekend in Minnesota.

_____

_____

_____

_____

2. The family of wolves saw Pat and the other campers sitting by their campfire.

_____

_____

_____

_____

B. Read the paragraph below. Write a topic sentence that could go with it.

She rolled up the sleeping bags tightly. Pat and two other campers made sure the campfire was completely out. She also helped the others take down the tent and pack up the rest of the gear.

Topic Sentence:

_____

_____

HBJ material copyrighted under notice appearing earlier in this work.

64   *Main Idea and Details*   Practice Book ■ **EMERALD FOREST**

••• RUNNING WITH THE PACK •••

Name_____

Choose one of the activities below. Work by yourself or with a classmate to do the activity.

ACTIVITY 1

Now that you've read "Running With the Pack," make a new K-W-L chart. List what you now know about wolves and what you would still like to find out. Then read more about wolves in encyclopedias or other books, and fill in the last column on your chart with what you learned. Share your chart with your classmates.

ACTIVITY 2

Make a map to show where wolves live today. Use a K-W-L chart to organize your research. List what you know about where wolves live and what you would still like to know. After you research the subject in the library, add what you have learned to the chart. Then make your map and display it in the classroom.

ACTIVITY 3

Research another member of the dog family, such as the coyote, fox, jackal, or dingo. Make a K-W-L chart to organize your ideas and your knowledge. Report to the group on what you learn.

Name _____

Read the words in the chart. Then use them to complete the paragraphs below. You may use each word more than once.

Nouns	disguise	avalanche	
Adjectives	baffled	logical	weird

Mario's Plant

I know that Mario likes unusual plants, but his newest one

is downright _____. Every ten days it drops an
         (adjective)

_____ of leaves onto the floor, which Mario and I
    (noun)

have to sweep up. Then, it grows all its leaves back. I helped Mario

search through many books to find a _____ explanation
                            (adjective)

for this. After searching for three weeks, however, we are still

_____.
   (adjective)

Julie's Costume

Julie was completely _____ about what to wear to the
             (adjective)

costume party. Then she had a bright idea! Since her favorite food was

salad and her favorite animal was the rabbit, she thought that a giant

carrot would be the most _____ _____.
                           (adjective)   (noun)

Julie described her costume to her mother, who listened patiently to

this _____ explanation. She said that Julie should definitely
    (adjective)

win a prize but she wasn't sure for what.

••• THE PLANT THAT ATE DIRTY SOCKS •••

Name _____

A. Complete the story map below.

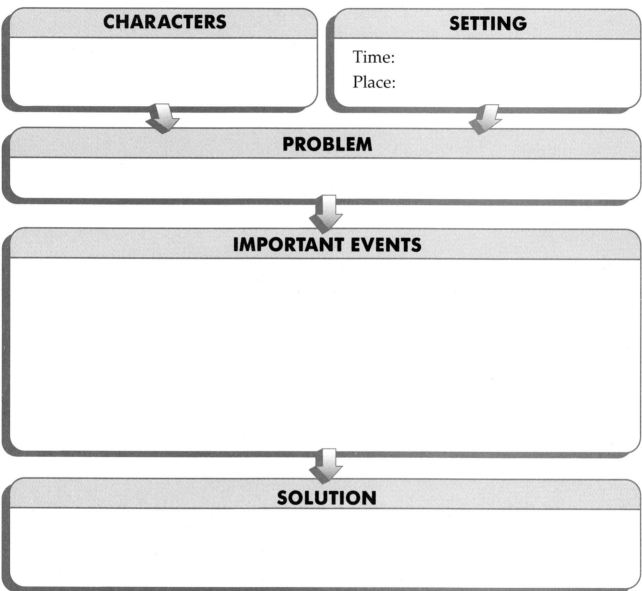

B. Use your story map to write a brief summary of the selection.

_____

_____

_____

Summarizing the Literature

• • • THE PLANT THAT ATE DIRTY SOCKS • • •

Name _____

A. Read each sentence below. Then write the same sentence, using a synonym of the word in dark print. Draw a line around the synonym you use.

1. Michael's vines got **thicker** than Norman's.

_____

2. Michael thought Norman was **swiping** his socks.

_____

3. Michael **yanked** the closet door open.

_____

4. The socks had **vanished** during the night.

_____

B. Complete each sentence, using an antonym of the word in dark print.

1. The new plants looked very **weird**, compared to the old

plants, which looked quite _____.

2. Michael had some **messy** growing methods, but Norman's

methods were very _____.

3. Michael tried to **remember** not to scratch his nose, but he

_____ this when his nose itched.

4. At night Michael **locked** his door, and in the morning he

_____ it.

HBJ material copyrighted under notice appearing earlier in this work.

---

68   **Synonyms/Antonyms**   Practice Book ▪ **EMERALD FOREST**

• • • THE PLANT THAT ATE DIRTY SOCKS • • •

Name_____

A. Read the paragraph below. Pay careful attention to the underlined words.

     Sequoia was a member of the Cherokee nation. Sequoia developed a written alphabet for his people. <u>He</u> is also remembered because of the trees that bear his name. Sequoia trees are some of the largest and oldest living things on Earth. <u>They</u> can live for several thousand years! The General Sherman Tree in Sequoia National Park is one of the world's tallest trees. <u>It</u> is 272.4 feet tall.

B. Write the underlined subject pronouns in the first column below. Then write the word or words each pronoun replaces.

     Subject Pronoun   **Replaces**

_____   _____

_____   _____

_____   _____

Imagine that you are a scientist studying sequoia trees. Write a few sentences that you might include in your field notes. Use at least three subject pronouns.

_____

_____

• •

SUMMARIZING
the **L**EARNING   A word that takes the place of one or more nouns and is used as the

subject of a sentence is called a _____ . Singular subject pronouns

are _____ . Plural subject pronouns are _____ .

Name _____

A. Read the paragraph below. Then add time-order words to help signal the order of events.

_____, Michael saw an advertisement on a cereal box for "Amazing Beans." _____, he cut out the order form. _____, Michael carefully completed the form. _____, he addressed an envelope, inserted the form, and stamped it. _____, Michael mailed the order form.

B. Michael and Norman had a very messy closet. If you were in their place, what steps would you take to clean it? Write a paragraph in which you describe what you would do. Use time-order words to signal the order of events.

_____

_____

_____

_____

_____

_____

SUMMARIZING *the* **L**EARNING   Time-order words, such as _____,

_____, _____, _____, and

_____, help me figure out the

_____ of events in a story.

• • • THE PLANT THAT ATE DIRTY SOCKS • • •

Name _____

Complete the charts below with causes or effects.

Effects
The boys clean their room.
Norman inspects the closet.
Michael suspects a thief.

Cause

Cause
Michael conducts an experiment.

Effects

SUMMARIZING *the* **L**EARNING   When I read, I ask myself what is happening. This is called the _____. Then I ask myself why this has happened. The reason is the _____.

• • • CARNIVOROUS PLANTS • • •

Name _____

Read the words in the box. Think about what each word
means. Then complete each paragraph, using words from the
box. Use each word only once.

immediately	nectar	exotic	rare
environment	substance	preserve	carbon dioxide

Not long ago, concern about the loss of forested lands was

_____. Now people know how important forests are.

Trees use _____ _____, a gas produced by humans
and animals, to make oxygen. Forests also provide an

_____ that many kinds of animals need to
survive. Some governments have passed laws to

_____ forests so that future
generations can enjoy them, too.

People interested in _____ plants that they had
never seen before went to the flower show. Most visitors were

_____ attracted to the purple, red, and white
orchids. Some people listened to a beekeeper talk about her job
of raising honeybees. She explained that flowering plants

produce a sweet-smelling _____ that attracts

bees. Bees use this liquid, called _____, to make
honey.

• • • CARNIVOROUS PLANTS • • •

Name _____

A. One way to summarize a nonfiction selection is to complete a
K-W-L chart. Use the chart below to summarize what you learn.

K What I Know	W What I Want to Know	L What I Learned

B. Write one sentence that tells what you learned about carnivorous plants.

_____

_____

• • • CARNIVOROUS PLANTS • • •

Name _____

The words below are from the selection. Read each word, and then read the headings in the boxes that follow. Write each word in the appropriate box.

energy	plankton	nectar	gland
minerals	tendril	cilia	nitrogen
passive	bladder	larvae	active
digestive enzymes		carbon dioxide	

Fluids Produced by Carnivorous Plants

Elements Needed by Plants to Make Food

Words That Describe Plants' Traps

Very Tiny Living Things

Parts of Carnivorous Plants' Traps

Name_____

A. Read the paragraphs below, and circle the object
pronoun used in place of a noun in each paragraph.
Use the list of object pronouns to help you.

OBJECT PRONOUNS
me
you
him
her
it
us
them

Curare is a powerful poison made from plants. People
have many uses for it.

Years ago, curare was used on the tips of arrows by
some South American tribes. The poison was an important
hunting tool for them.

These days, if patients need to sleep during an operation,
a doctor might give them a drug that is made from curare.

B. Complete the sentences below.

In the first paragraph, the object pronoun _____ replaces *curare.*

In the second paragraph, the object pronoun *them* replaces

_____ .

In the third paragraph, the object pronoun *them* replaces _____ .

Write a sentence or two about the importance of plants.
Use at least one singular and one plural object pronoun.

_____

_____

SUMMARIZING
the **L**EARNING   A word that takes the place of one or more nouns and is used as

the object of a sentence is called an _____ . _____

_____ are the singular object pronouns. _____

are the plural object pronouns.

CARNIVOROUS PLANTS

Name_____

A. Each word in the roots of the tree matches one of the
clues below. Write the word beside the clue.
Use the information in the chart to help you.

Greek Roots	Latin Roots
metron ("measure")	*vorare* ("to eat")
bios ("life")	*omnis* ("all")
graphein ("to write")	*herba* ("plant")
tele ("far away")	*centum* ("hundred")
hydra ("water")	
skopein ("look at")	
chronos ("time")	

omnivore   telegraph   telescope   centimeter

1. This word means "someone who eats both
   plants and meat."   _____

2. This allows you to write to people
   far away.   _____

3. This allows you to look at something
   far away.   _____

4. This is a unit of measurement that is $\frac{1}{100}$ of a meter.   _____

CARNIVOROUS PLANTS

Name_____

B. Write a synonym or an explanation for each word below. If you need more information, use the chart on page 76 or a dictionary.

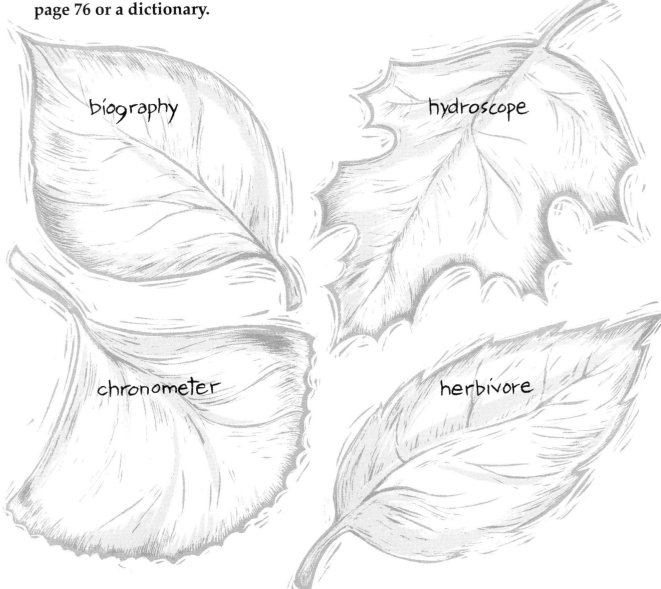

biography

hydroscope

chronometer

herbivore

With your classmates, make a chart of any words with Greek or Latin roots that you discover in your reading. Add to the chart throughout the school year. Display the chart in your classroom.

Name _____

Use the SQ3R strategy to study the paragraphs and answer the questions.

Survey

1. What do you learn from the headings? _____

2. How do the pictures help you predict what the selection will

be about? _____

Question

3. Write three questions about the headings.

    a. _____

    b. _____

    c. _____

Read   Read the article to answer your questions.

PLANT RESPONSES

Plants respond in various ways to what is around them. Of course, plants respond more slowly than animals to their environment, so they are harder to observe. But you may notice three main plant responses to light, gravity, and water. These responses help the plant get what it needs to survive.

Response to Light

Imagine that you are growing plants in artificial light. If one day you moved the light source, within a few days you would notice that the plant's leaves had slowly turned toward the new position of the light.

Plants need light to grow. They use the light of the sun in their food-making process, photosynthesis. Without light, a plant would die. For this reason, plant stems usually grow upward toward the light. This plant response is called **heliotropism**.

CARNIVOROUS PLANTS

Name _____

Response to Gravity

If you turned a potted plant upside down, after some time you would notice that the roots had begun to grow back toward the ground.

It is important that plants stay rooted firmly in the ground. For this reason, roots usually grow downward, into the earth. This plant response is called **geotropism.**

Response to Water

If you stopped watering some of your plants, soon you would notice that the leaves of your plants had begun to dry out. If you continued to withhold water, the plants would die.

Plants need water to live. Therefore, their roots will grow toward underground water supplies. This plant response is called **hydrotropism.**

heliotropism

geotropism

hydrotropism

Recite

4. As you were reading the selection, what answers to your questions did you find?

a. _____

b. _____

c. _____

Review

5. Why should you review what you learned from reading?

_____

_____

••• CARNIVOROUS PLANTS •••

Name_____

Ahmad was absent when your class learned how to take notes. Read the information in the passage below. Then show Ahmad how to take notes by completing the note card.

You'll never see a real dinosaur, but you can see the same kind of tree that dinosaurs saw. The ginkgo tree lived millions of years ago, and ginkgoes are common today. Ginkgoes are tall, slender trees with fan-shaped leaves. The fruit looks something like a plum and contains a nut that can be eaten once it has been roasted. You might even find a ginkgo tree in your own town. Many cities plant them because they look decorative.

— *Ancient Trees* by J. L. Rolfe. Centerville Publishers, 1992.

Main Idea: _____
_____

Details: _____
_____
_____
_____

Source: _____

With a partner, find out more about unusual plants by reading encyclopedia articles or other reference books. You might even read a gardening magazine to find out about unusual plants you can grow. Take notes as you read. Share with your classmates what you have learned.

THE GREAT KAPOK TREE

Name _____

Help Lucy edit her news article by replacing each underlined phrase
with a word from below. Write each new word above the phrase.

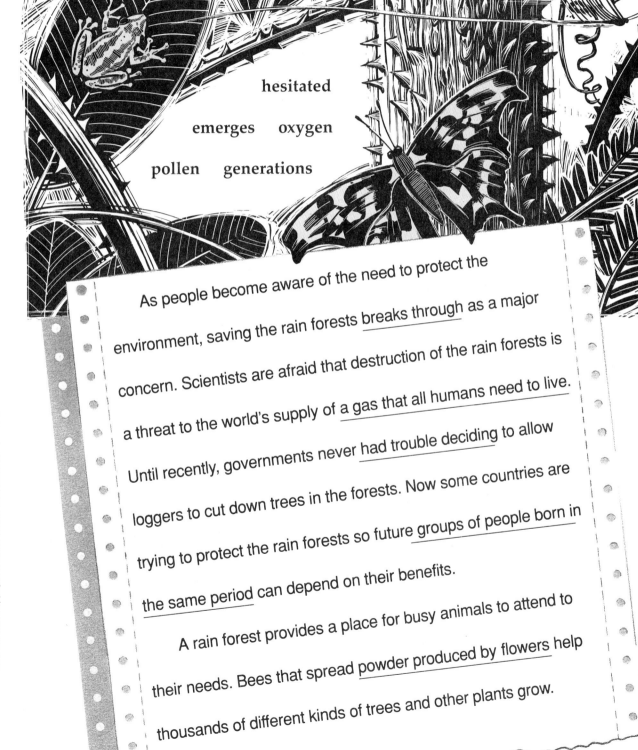

hesitated

emerges   oxygen

pollen   generations

As people become aware of the need to protect the

environment, saving the rain forests <u>breaks through</u> as a major

concern. Scientists are afraid that destruction of the rain forests is

a threat to the world's supply of <u>a gas that all humans need to live.</u>

Until recently, governments <u>never had trouble deciding</u> to allow

loggers to cut down trees in the forests. Now some countries are

trying to protect the rain forests so future <u>groups of people born in</u>

<u>the same period</u> can depend on their benefits.

    A rain forest provides a place for busy animals to attend to

their needs. Bees that spread <u>powder produced by flowers</u> help

thousands of different kinds of trees and other plants grow.

Name _____

A. One way to summarize a story is to analyze important details.
Complete the story map below.

> Setting:

> Characters:

> Problem:

> Event 1:
>
> Event 2:
>
> Event 3:
>
> Event 4:
>
> Event 5:

> Solution:

B. Use your story map to write a one-sentence summary about the
story.

_____

_____

Name _____

Write a paragraph describing what you would see and hear if you were the girl in the illustration below. Use words that sound like their meanings.

_____

_____

_____

_____

_____

THE GREAT KAPOK TREE

Name_____

A. Read the paragraph below. Pay careful attention to the underlined words.

What do gorillas, tigers, and pandas have in common? They are all endangered species. Many animals face extinction because <u>their</u> numbers have become very small. But some people are taking steps to keep them from disappearing completely. To find out more about these efforts, visit <u>your</u> local library and ask the librarian for help. <u>His</u> or <u>her</u> advice will get you started.

B. To whom does each underlined word refer?

<u>Their</u> refers to _____.

<u>Your</u> refers to _____.

<u>His</u> or <u>her</u> refers to _____.

Use the lines below to write two sentences about the animals of the rain forest. Use at least two possessive pronouns.

_____

_____

_____

SUMMARIZING *the* **L**EARNING Words that take the place of possessive nouns are called

_____. Some possessive pronouns are _____

_____. Some possessive pronouns appear before a

noun. Others _____.

Practice Book ■ **EMERALD FOREST**

THE GREAT KAPOK TREE

Name _____

A. Study the city map of São Paulo below. Then answer the questions that follow.

1. Which coordinates can you use to tell a classmate where the

   São Paulo Museum of Art is located? _____

2. What route would you follow to travel from the São Paulo

   Museum of Art to Morumbi Stadium? _____

   _____

3. What major site can you locate by using the coordinates B 3?

   _____

4. Which coordinates can you use to tell where the Parque da

   Independencia is located? _____

5. What park might you visit if you went to the area with

   coordinates C 3? _____

THE GREAT KAPOK TREE

Name _____

B. Study the table of information about the longest rivers in the world. Then answer the questions below.

Longest Rivers of the World		
Name	**Miles in Length**	**Location**
Amazon	4,000	South America
Congo	2,900	Africa
Huang Ho	2,903	China
Mekong	2,600	Asia
Mississippi	2,348	United States
Missouri	2,315	United States
Niger	2,600	Africa
Nile	4,145	Africa
Volga	2,193	Eastern Europe
Yangtze	3,915	China

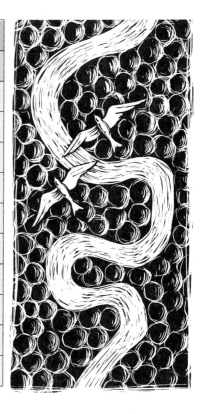

1. Which river is the longest river in the world? _____

How long is it? _____ Where would you find

this river? _____

2. Which river is the second longest river in the world?

_____ How long is it? _____

3. Which rivers are located in China, and how long are they? _____

_____

4. How much longer is the Amazon than the Mississippi? _____

5. Where would you travel to see the Volga River? _____

• • • THE GREAT KAPOK TREE • • •

Name _____

Read the paragraphs, and then answer the questions that follow.

It had been more than a year since Kareem had moved
away from Springfield. He wondered if the tree he had planted
last spring had grown much. He decided to call Carla that night
to find out.

After dinner, he called Carla. Her mother answered and said
that Carla had just left but would be back soon. Within an hour,
Carla called Kareem back. After a few minutes of chitchat,
Kareem got to the point.

"How's my lemon tree doing?" he asked.

"It's doing fine," she said. "I've been watering it
every day. I think we'll have some lemons soon."

1. What words tell you how long ago Kareem left Springfield? _____

_____

2. If it was 7:30 when Kareem first called Carla's house, was it before

or after 8:30 when Carla called back? How do you know? _____

_____

3. How long did Kareem talk to Carla before he asked about his

lemon tree? _____

4. What words tell you when Kareem planted the lemon tree? _____

5. Kareem decided to call Carla that night. What did he do before he

called? _____

••• THE GREAT KAPOK TREE •••

Name_____

A. Read the passage below. Then complete the chart about the causes and effects.

Many of the trees in the forest had been chopped down. Plants that needed some shade and a great deal of moisture were exposed to too much sun. When it rained that winter, much of the topsoil was washed away because there were no plants to hold it in place. New seeds couldn't take root in the sandy soil that was left.

Scientists began to plant new trees in parts of the forest. As the years went by, some shade-loving plants began to grow there again. Even some animals that had left the forest began to return.

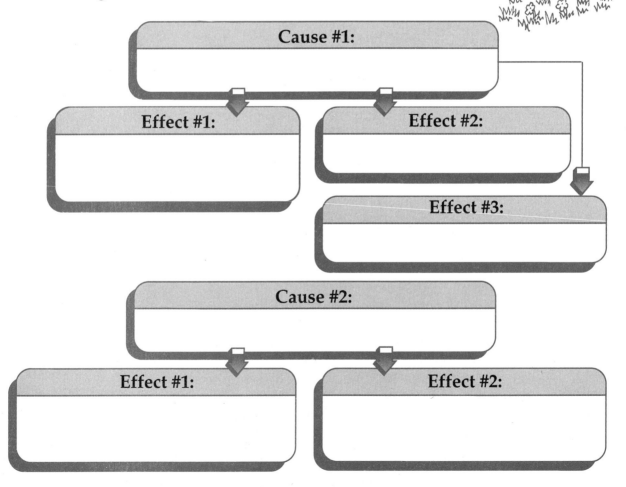

Cause #1:

Effect #1:

Effect #2:

Effect #3:

Cause #2:

Effect #1:

Effect #2:

THE GREAT KAPOK TREE

Name_____

B. Choose one of the following activities. Work by yourself or with a classmate to complete the activity.

Activity 1

Reread "The Great Kapok Tree." Make a chart showing that one cause can have many effects. First, list the name of each animal that speaks to the man. Also include the child who speaks. The cause for each character is the same: If the Kapok tree is chopped down. Write the effects that each animal and the child say will happen if the man chops down the Kapok tree. Display your chart in the classroom.

Activity 3

Create a graphic organizer, such as a web, a chart, or a diagram. Use it to compare and contrast the causes and effects of too *much* rainfall for a long period of time and too *little* rainfall for a long period of time. Before you begin your organizer, you may want to list the effects of too much rain and too little rain. Add a caption, and display your graphic organizer on a bulletin board.

Activity 2

Write three paragraphs telling what would happen if all the trees in your neighborhood were destroyed. Include the effects on you, your parents, your neighbors, and other people and animals in your neighborhood. Share your paragraphs with your classmates.

••• DOWN UNDER, DOWN UNDER •••

Name_____

Use the words below to complete the sentences or
answer the clues.

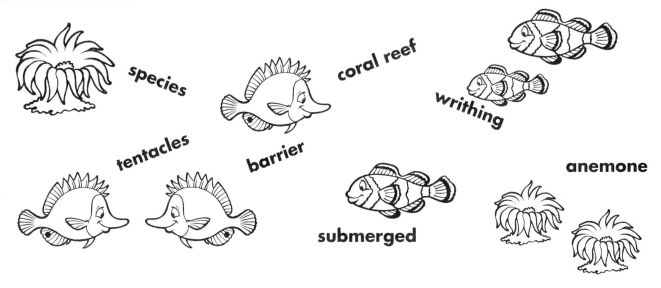

species coral reef writhing

tentacles barrier anemone

submerged

1. This sea creature has a tube-shaped body. _____

2. Many different _____ of fish live in the ocean.

3. This is a ledge found in shallow water. It is made of the skeletons

   of tiny sea animals. _____

4. A diver needs an air tank to remain under water, or _____,
   for very long.

5. These look like long, waving fingers. _____

6. This is something that blocks movement. _____

7. *Twisting* and *squirming* mean the same as this word. _____

With your classmates, make a mural showing the Great Barrier Reef. How
many kinds of sea creatures can you draw and label? You might want to use
an encyclopedia for help.

Name_____

A. One way to summarize a selection is to create a concept map. Complete the map below, recording important details from "Down Under, Down Under."

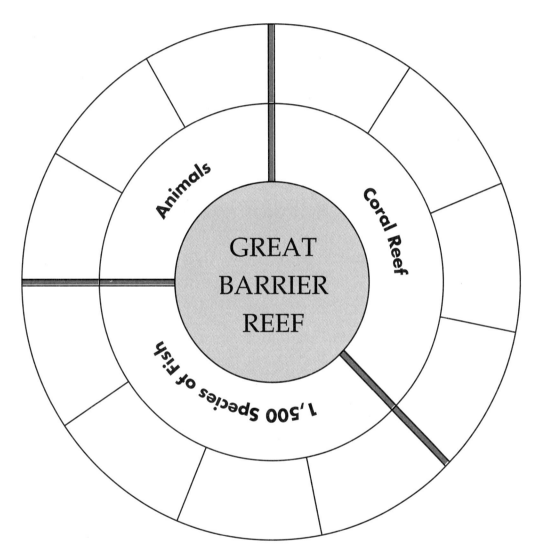

B. Use the information in your chart to write a brief summary of the selection.

_____

_____

_____

Name_____

A. Read the paragraph below. Then circle each adjective
and draw a square around each article.

Some adventurous people dive to see the wonderful creatures

that live near a reef. Diving requires special equipment, including a

mask, a tank, and a device called a *regulator* that controls the air the diver

receives. Divers must take training because serious injury can result

if they come up from deep water quickly.

B. Circle the adjective or adjectives that describe each
underlined noun. Then draw an arrow from the
adjective to the noun it describes. Finally, draw a
square around each article.

An octopus is a creature that you might see while diving. An octopus

has a soft <u>body</u>, large <u>eyes</u>, and eight long <u>arms</u>. Many <u>kinds</u> of octopuses

can be found on the muddy <u>bottoms</u> of shallow <u>parts</u> of the ocean.

Write a sentence that describes an undersea scene.
Be sure to include at least one adjective and one article.

_____

_____

SUMMARIZING
the **L**EARNING   An _____ is a word that describes a noun or a

pronoun. The articles _____ , _____ , and _____ are special adjectives.

• • • Down Under, Down Under • • •

Name _____

A. Read the set of directions below. Then add time-order words
that will make the directions easier to understand.

_____, it is a good idea to get to the
theater on time if you want to see a good movie.

_____, you stand in line to buy your ticket.

_____ you get inside, you may want to buy some
popcorn or a drink. If so, you must stand in another line.

_____, treats in hand, you can try to find a good

seat. _____, you are ready to sit down
and enjoy the show.

B. The sentences in the directions below are out of order. Find the
time-order words, and draw a line around them. On another
sheet of paper, rewrite the directions, using the time-order
words as clues to the correct order.

Next, you straighten the bedspread. Then, you pull
up the top sheet and tuck it in. First, you smooth out the
bottom sheet and tuck it in. After tucking in the top
sheet, you straighten the blanket and tuck it in. Finally,
you pull the bedspread over the pillows and tuck it neatly
under the pillows. Then, you put the pillows on top of
the blanket.

• • • Down Under, Down Under • • •

Name_____

C. Study the pictures showing the steps to follow to wrap a gift. Then write the steps in order. Use the time-order words in the box.

1.  **2.** 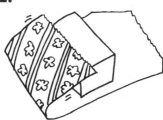 **3.**

4.  **5.**

then	first	finally	next	second

_____
_____
_____
_____

 **W**ith a group of classmates, make a handbook to give to new students at your school. Include directions to follow in case of fire or other emergencies.

Name_____

Read the sample test below. **DO NOT answer the test questions.**

A. **Read each question. Circle the best answer.**

    1. Where is the Great Barrier Reef?

        near South America   near Africa

    2. What material makes up the Great Barrier Reef?

        sand   sharks

B. **Read each question. Write the answer on the back of this sheet.**

    1. What is a *polyp*?

    2. How does the anemone protect the clown fish?

C. **Read each statement. Write *T* if it is true. Write *F* if it is false.**

    1. Most nudibranchs are no larger than two inches. _____

    2. Nudibranch means "no branches." _____

Now, answer these questions about the test.

Which part of the test would take the most time to complete, and why?

_____

_____

If you don't know the answer to a question on a test, what should you do?

_____

If you have extra time at the end of the test, what should you do?

_____

••• DOWN UNDER, DOWN UNDER •••

Name_____

Yvette read an article about divers who search for sunken treasure. Now she is having trouble putting the steps of the search in the correct order. Read the paragraph and then write your answers to Yvette's questions.

Did you know that treasure hunters sometimes find gold on the ocean floor? Teams of divers search for the remains of Spanish ships that sank hundreds of years ago while carrying gold from the Americas. It's not easy to find a sunken wreck. First, the divers spend months studying old documents in libraries, trying to find records of a sinking. Then they fly over certain places in the ocean, looking for shapes in the water that might indicate a wreck. Next, they use scientific instruments to scan the ocean floor, looking for metal objects. After they find a sunken ship, they make careful drawings or photographs of the whole area to help them keep track of what they find.

Questions		Answers
What is the first thing divers do if they want to find a sunken ship?		
When do they use instruments to scan the ocean floor?		
Which do the divers do first, scan the area with instruments or take photographs?		

••• DOWN UNDER, DOWN UNDER •••

Name_____

The students in Mr. Blake's class have made a list of questions about coral reefs. Help them decide where to find the information they need. Write *encyclopedia, dictionary,* or *atlas* beside each question.

QUESTIONS	REFERENCE SOURCE
1. What are the three kinds of coral reefs?	
2. What are the main differences between a barrier reef and an atoll?	
3. What does the word lagoon mean?	
4. How far is it from Brisbane, Australia, to the southern tip of the Great Barrier Reef?	
5. What is the pronunciation of algae?	
6. What human activities are harmful to coral reefs?	
7. Is the word cerata a noun or an adjective?	
8. What effect do starfish have on coral reefs?	
9. Which Florida city is the nearest to John Pennekamp Coral Reef State Park?	

ACTIVITY CORNER

With a group of classmates, make a bulletin board display about coral reefs. Use encyclopedias, atlases, and dictionaries to help you find the information you need.

Name _____

Read the following story. Use clues in the story to figure out the meaning of each underlined word. Then write each word on the line next to its meaning.

    Long ago, the Ogata family packed up everything, moved to South Dakota, and bought some land. They planned to farm the hundred acres of land and live there forever. Sadly, they had two seasons of bad crops and ran out of money. The bank threatened to foreclose on their property.

    One night, three children from a neighboring farm were up to mischief. Wandering around the Ogatas' farm by the light of a lantern, they found an old mine shaft. They told the Ogatas about their startling discovery. The Ogatas owned a gold mine!

    Mr. and Mrs. Ogata checked the deed to their property carefully. They were afraid they would find a loophole that would force them to give up their claim to the mine. But the mine was theirs. The day the first ore was mined, the Ogatas gave each of the three children ten gold nuggets.

1. _____ a protective case to hold a light

2. _____ a legal document showing ownership of property

3. _____ measures of land with a certain area

4. _____ a way of getting out of the intended meaning of a law or agreement

5. _____ to take away the right to own property

6. _____ behavior that may cause trouble

7. _____ causing sharp surprise

Name _____

A. Complete the story map below.

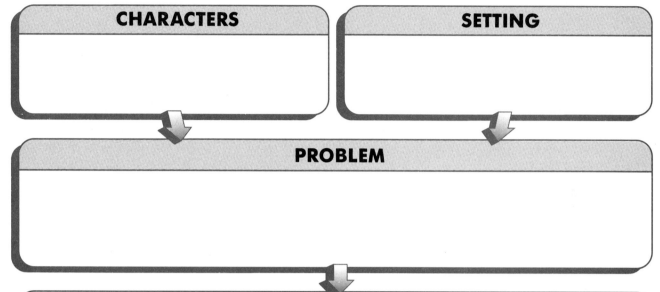

CHARACTERS

SETTING

PROBLEM

IMPORTANT EVENTS

OUTCOME

B. Write a one-sentence summary of the story.

_____

_____

_____

 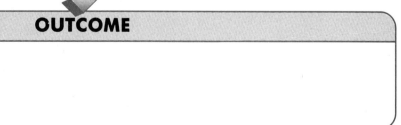

Name_____

A. Read the paragraph below about the McBrooms' farm. Circle all the adjectives that make comparisons.

You have to be careful at the McBrooms' farm. The weeds grow thicker and taller than anywhere else. The corn is more dangerous than the weeds. Cornstalks can shoot up and skin your nose! And the banana squash grow the fastest of all.

B. Write the correct form of the adjectives in parentheses.

At first, the McBrooms' farm was _____ (muddier/muddiest) than the neighboring farms. Then came the _____ (dry/driest) hot spell ever. Soon the McBrooms had the _____ (richer/richest) soil in the area. Mr. Heck Jones thought he was _____ (smart/smarter) than Josh McBroom, but he was really the (more/most) _____ foolish man of all.

Use some adjectives to write a sentence comparing a garden you have seen to the McBrooms' farm.

_____

_____

•••
SUMMARIZING
the **L**EARNING Adjectives with the endings _____ and _____ are used to compare things. Add _____ to most adjectives to compare two things. Add _____ to most adjectives to compare more than two things.

Name _____

Read each example of figurative language below. Under each one, draw a line around the sentence that means about the same as the example. Then write the same idea in your own words, using figurative language.

1. "That pond bottom felt as soft and rich as black silk."

It was expensive.   It was good, dark farmland.

_____

_____

2. "I was in a sudden fever of excitement."

I suddenly felt ill.   I was excited suddenly.

_____

_____

3. "That glorious topsoil seemed to cry out for seed."

It was ready for seeds.   It was wet with tears.

_____

_____

4. "The stalk shot up so fast it would skin your nose."

It grew very rapidly.   It was dangerous.

_____

_____

SUMMARIZING *the* **L**EARNING   Writers use _____ to add humor, make comparisons, and hold the reader's interest.

• • • McBROOM TELLS THE TRUTH • • •

Name _____

Use this map to provide directions for each situation.

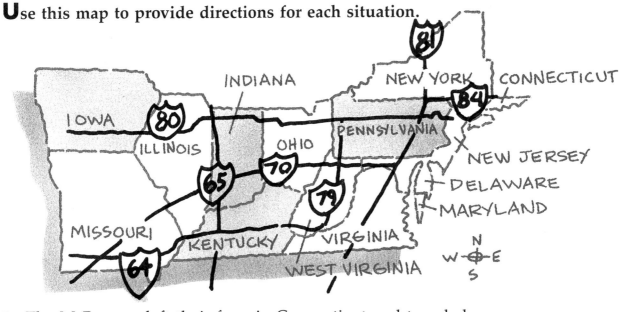

1. The McBrooms left their farm in Connecticut and traveled
west to Iowa. Write directions for them to follow.

_____

_____

_____

2. Choose one step in your directions, and write what would
happen if the McBrooms didn't follow that step.

_____

_____

3. Write directions telling the McBrooms how they could avoid
going through Ohio on their way to Iowa.

_____

_____

_____

Name _____

Read each pair of sentences below. Draw a line around the cause, and underline the effect. Then write a sentence that tells a new effect that might be caused by the one you underlined. The first one is done for you.

1. (Ronnie went to the beach.) <u>Ronnie got a sunburn.</u>

   New effect: ___Ronnie started peeling two days later._____

2. The McBrooms stay up late. They oversleep the next morning.

   New effect: _____

3. Heck plants weed seeds. Heck wants to drive the McBrooms away.

   New effect: _____

4. The moths think it is night. It is very dark in the pine forest.

   New effect: _____

5. The pine trees grow very close together. No sun can get through.

   New effect: _____

6. There have been many fish in the lake. The soil at the
   bottom of the pond is rich in nitrogen.

   New effect: _____

7. The children dive into the mud. The pond dries up very fast.

   New effect: _____

8. Heck Jones's land is extremely hard. A tornado has carried off
   all of Heck Jones's topsoil.

   New effect: _____

Name _____

A. **Read each sentence below. Figure out the meaning of the underlined word. Then write the word on the line next to its meaning.**

1. A <u>stampede</u> of people ran from their homes hoping to find safety near the shore.

2. Burning pieces of rock burst out of the top of the <u>volcano</u>.

3. About every one hundred years, the mountain <u>erupts</u> and blackens the air with smoke and ashes.

4. The boiling <u>lava</u> that flowed down the slope of the mountain sent up clouds of steam.

5. Rescue workers suffered from <u>exhaustion</u> after many days of hard work.

6. Their sleep was <u>interrupted</u> by reports of new tremors in a nearby town.

a. _____ state of being very tired

b. _____ mountain that may throw out hot rocks

c. _____ very hot liquified rock

d. _____ sudden rushing away because of panic

e. _____ stopped by breaking in

f. _____ throws out hot rocks

B. **On another sheet of paper, write a story about a volcano, using at least four of the following words:** *exhaustion, interrupted, lava, stampede, volcano, erupts.*

Name _____

A. One way to summarize a story is to complete a cause-and-effect chain. Use the one below.

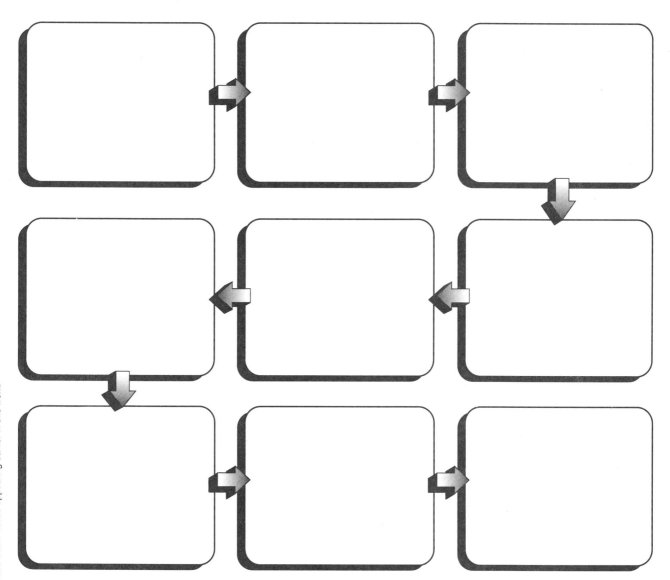

B. Use the information in your cause-and-effect chain to write a brief summary of the story.

_____

_____

_____

Name _____

Peter gets bitten by a tsetse fly and contracts sleeping sickness.
Read about this disease in the paragraphs below. Then draw a line
under the best ending to each sentence that follows.

Sleeping sickness is a **serious disease** of tropical
Africa. It is caused by a **protozoan** that can get into a
person's body through a tsetse fly's bite. Once this single-
celled animal is inside a person's body, it multiplies
rapidly. The disease quickly spreads throughout the body,
eventually reaching the brain.

In most cases, a complete **cure** is possible if the
disease is treated before it reaches the brain. If left
untreated, the disease will cause a **coma,** or loss of
consciousness, and death.

1. Another word for *serious* is _____.
certain   dangerous
painless   slow

2. Another word for *disease* is _____.
coma   measles
illness   health

3. A protozoan is a _____.
noisy creature   sneaky creature
single-celled animal   dangerous insect

4. If a person is in a coma, he or she _____.
can talk but can't walk   is unconscious
can hear but not see   is cold

5. A cure is a _____.
successful treatment   shot
bath   bug spray

Name_____

A. Read the paragraph below. Circle each action verb.
Underline each linking verb.

Last summer my friends and I invented a game
called "Quick Changes." In this game we write
the names of real or imaginary creatures on slips of
paper. Each player takes a slip. For ten minutes, each
player is the animal on the slip. For example, I was
a seal one morning. I flopped around in the wading
pool. I barked. I splashed water at my friends.

B. Use a form of the linking verb *be* to complete each sentence.

1. José and I _____ eager to play the new game.

2. "Oh, boy! I _____ an eagle!" says José.

3. "_____ you ready for your turn?" asks Sara.

4. Maria _____ a bat, hanging from a tree branch.

5. Some of my friends _____ really silly.

6. "This _____ a very strange game!" says José's sister.

Write a few sentences about a game you and your friends
enjoy. Use at least one action verb and one linking verb.

_____

_____

SUMMARIZING
the **L**EARNING   Verbs that tell what the subject of a sentence *does* or *did* are

called _____. Verbs that tell what the subject of a sentence *is* or *is*

like are called _____.

Name _____

Read each group of sentences. Put a check mark next to the conclusion or conclusions you can draw from each group. Then answer the question that follows.

1. Father tucked his scarf inside his coat. Mother pinned her hat in place. They asked the children to keep the house neat.

   ____ The parents are going out for a while.

   ____ The parents will eat dinner in a restaurant.

   ____ The children are old enough to be left alone.

   What real-life experiences helped you decide which

   conclusions were valid? _____

   _____

2. It was cold for November. The children could see their breath like steam. They rolled in the leaves.

   ____ It is usually warmer in November than described here.

   ____ It is usually colder in November than described here.

   ____ The leaves have fallen from the trees.

   What real-life experiences helped you decide which

   conclusions were valid? _____

   _____

SUMMARIZING the LEARNING I use _____ and _____

_____ to draw a valid conclusion.

JUMANJI

Name _____

A. Look at Grid A below. Put your pen or pencil at point A-1
(where the *X* is), and draw lines as directed.

Go up one space to B-1. Go right one space to B-2.
Go up one space to C-2. Go right one space to C-3.
Go up one space to D-3. Go right one space to D-4.
Go up one space to E-4. Go right one space to E-5.
Go up one space to F-5. Go right one space to F-6.
Go up one space to G-6. Go right one space to G-7.
Go down six spaces to A-7. Go left six spaces to A-1.

What does the figure look like? _____

B. Draw a design on Grid B below, using only straight lines.
Then write a set of directions that explains how you drew
your design.

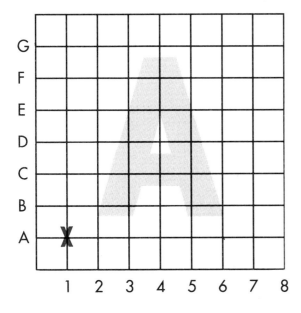 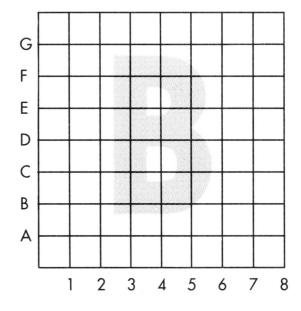

Directions: _____

_____

_____

Name _____

A. **Read each question, and think about where you might find the answer. Then write *encyclopedia* or *dictionary* on the line.**

1. What does the word *melody* mean? _____

2. What kind of a childhood did Abraham Lincoln have? _____

3. What happened during the Industrial Revolution? _____

4. What is the root word for *hypothermia*? _____

5. What are some synonyms for *good-looking*? _____

6. What was the birthplace of Martin Luther King, Jr.? _____

7. What is the difference in meaning between *forceful* and *pushy*? _____

8. What does the abbreviation *ibid.* mean? _____

9. What kinds of chemicals are used in developing photographs

 from negatives? _____

10. What is the history of the ballet? _____

Name _____

B. Read each entry. Where would you see such an entry—in an encyclopedia or in a dictionary? Write the answer on the line.

1. in·got [ing′gət] *n.* A mass of metal cast into the shape of a

bar or block. _____

2. The original Luddites were followers of a legendary Ned Ludd. These 19th-century British laborers smashed textile-

making machines that threatened their jobs. _____

3. India is a republic in southern Asia. Its largest city is

Calcutta, and its capital is New Delhi. _____

4. hot air *informal* Empty, boastful talk. _____

5. ə = a in *above*, e in *sicken*, i in *possible*, o in *melon*,

u in *circus* _____

C. In the left column are entry words. In the right column are guide words that might be found on the same page in a dictionary. Write the letter of the guide words on the line next to the corresponding entry word.

1. _____ fortunate   **a.** gymnastics   gyve

2. _____ gypsum   **b.** node   nondescript

3. _____ nonchalant   **c.** forgetful   formulate

4. _____ normal   **d.** gung ho   gymnastic

5. _____ gutter   **e.** none   Norman

6. _____ formalize   **f.** formulation   foster

... CLOSE ENCOUNTER ...

OF A WEIRD KIND

Name _____

A. Read the words in the box. Think about what each word means. Then choose the word from the box that best completes the sentences below.

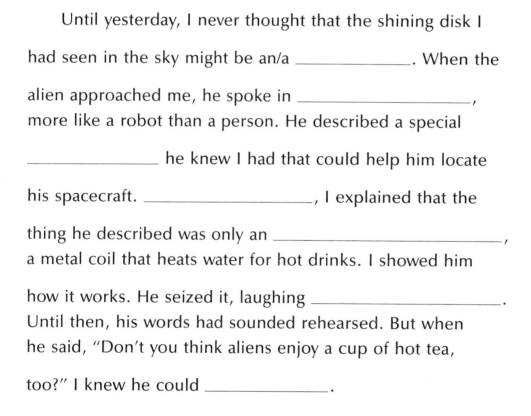

sheepishly	device	triumphantly
UFO	ad lib	monotones
	immersion heater	

Until yesterday, I never thought that the shining disk I

had seen in the sky might be an/a _____. When the

alien approached me, he spoke in _____,
more like a robot than a person. He described a special

_____ he knew I had that could help him locate

his spacecraft. _____, I explained that the

thing he described was only an _____,
a metal coil that heats water for hot drinks. I showed him

how it works. He seized it, laughing _____.
Until then, his words had sounded rehearsed. But when
he said, "Don't you think aliens enjoy a cup of hot tea,

too?" I knew he could _____.

B. On another sheet of paper, tell a story of your own in three or four sentences. Use at least four of the words from Part A.

Name _____

A. One way to summarize a play is to complete a problem-
solution map. Finish the one below by answering the
questions in the boxes.

Problem: What is the problem?

Solution: How do the children solve the problem?

Result: What happens after the Letonians leave?

B. Write a one-sentence summary of the selection, using
your problem-solution map.

_____

_____

_____

_____

CLOSE ENCOUNTER
OF A WEIRD KIND

Name _____

A. On each line provided, write the letter of the phrase that matches the abbreviation or acronym.

1. _____ AWOL   **a.** unidentified flying object

2. _____ NASA   **b.** disk operating system

3. _____ DOS   **c.** zone improvement plan

4. _____ RAM   **d.** absent without leave

5. _____ ZIP   **e.** random-access memory

6. _____ UFO   **f.** National Aeronautics and Space Administration

B. If the following were acronyms, what might they mean? Write a possible meaning on the line provided.

1. GLUB _____

2. DIRT _____

3. STAR _____

4. YSNOD _____

5. SMILE _____

C. Imagine that you and a group of your friends think you see some UFOs and have a "close encounter" with some alien creatures. You want to start a club for people who claim to have had similar experiences. On another sheet of paper, design an advertisement inviting people to join this club. Make up an appropriate acronym for your club's name.

Name_____

A. Read the paragraph below. Circle each main verb. Then draw an arrow from the helping verb to the main verb.

I am reading a book called *Planet 945.* My brother has read it, too! In the book, some pioneers are settling a new planet. No one has explored the planet yet, so they will have some amazing adventures there. In Chapter 4, two children are looking for a lost dog. They have discovered a ruined city.

B. Complete each sentence with a helping verb.

1. Kim and Ho _____ searching for the lost dog.

2. Kim _____ spotted a gleam between two hills.

3. "I _____ tired," Ho said.

4. "I _____ head for that valley," answered Kim. "You can rest here."

5. Ho _____ napping under a bush when Kim came back.

6. "Come and see. I _____ found the ruins of an old city!" she cried.

Write two sentences about a weird encounter.
Use a helping verb in each sentence.

_____

_____

••

SUMMARIZING *the* **L**EARNING The _____ is the most important verb in the sentence. A verb used with the main verb is called a _____ .

A helping verb shows _____ the action in a sentence happens.

···· CLOSE ENCOUNTER ····
OF A WEIRD KIND

Name _____

Read this chart of prefixes and suffixes and their meanings.

Prefix	Meaning	Suffix	Meaning
co-	"with another"	*-ly*	"in the manner of"
un-	"not"	*-ful*	"full of"
dis-	"not"	*-ian*	"from or of"
		-er	"one who"
		-tion	"the act of"

A. Add a prefix or a suffix to each underlined base word in parentheses to complete the sentences below. Write the new word on the line.

1. Mrs. Wilson told the children to be _____ to keep the door locked. (full of <u>care</u>)

2. They could _____ do that, the children said. (in an <u>easy</u> manner)

3. Later, however, the door was _____ because Jim put the cat out. (not <u>locked</u>)

4. A group of _____ landed in the back yard.

(beings from <u>Leto</u>)   Their _____ wanted them to get a special device from Earth. (one who <u>commands</u>)

5. The _____ said "thermos bottle" three times, to remember it. (one with the <u>captain</u>)

6. Mr. and Mrs. Wilson thought the children's stories came

from their _____. (acts of <u>imagining</u>)

7. The creatures were _____ with the immersion heater. (not <u>satisfied</u>)

116 | Structural Analysis

Practice Book ■ **EMERALD FOREST**

HBJ material copyrighted under notice appearing earlier in this work.

••• CLOSE ENCOUNTER •••
OF A WEIRD KIND

Name_____

B. The Letonians are just learning English. Study this chart, and then follow the directions below.

Prefix	Meaning	Suffix	Meaning
un- *im-* *mono-*	"not" "within, into" "one"	*-ion* *-ly*	"state, quality, or acting" "in a certain way"
Root	**Meaning**	**Root**	**Meaning**
notitia *quietus* *tonus*	"knowledge" "freedom from noise" "sound"	*mergere* *imaginare*	"to dip" "to picture in one's mind"

Use the chart to write meanings of these words for the Letonians.

quietly: _____

monotone: _____

immersion: _____

imagination: _____

What other words do you think the Letonians would like to take back with them? Get together with a partner and use the word parts on the chart to write a few more words—and their meanings—for the Letonians. Be creative, and give them some made-up words as well as real ones.

HBJ material copyrighted under notice appearing earlier in this work.

Name _____

The sentences below are taken from the story. Read them, and
then answer the questions that follow.

1. MRS. WILSON *(To MR. WILSON)*: I wouldn't be so worried if
we lived in town. Out here the nearest house is two miles away.

What does this tell the reader about the setting? _____

_____

_____

2. TOM *(Reassuringly)*: Sure, Mom. We understand. But we
really are old enough to take care of ourselves.

What does this tell the reader about Tom's character? _____

_____

_____

3. THERESA: It's O.K. We're safe. All the doors are locked.
JIM *(Sheepishly)*: They *were* locked. But remember when I put
out the cat?

What does this tell the reader about the characters? _____

_____

_____

4. 1ST LETONIAN: We are on a special mission. We have been
sent to bring something back from the earth to our planet.

What does this tell the reader about the plot? _____

_____

Name _____

Read the following sentences. Choose the word that best
completes the sentence, and write it on the line.

1. Anita wound up with a _____. With her on
second base, the baseball team almost had a chance.

     mystery   double   fly

2. It was clear that Alex wasn't paying attention after he

_____ every ball with the top of his
head. He seemed to forget that he had a mitt.

     fielded   solved   threw

3. Even though they lost, the team wasn't _____.
They knew they had played their best.

     jailed   talking   discouraged

4. The man was _____ by a woman who said she
saw him at the scene of the crime. It wasn't clear why she
had been in the area.

     accused   guilty   freed

5. The man said that he was _____. He also said
that he wasn't even in the country at the time.

     disguised   mysterious   innocent

6. Someone had planted evidence. The man was being

_____ for a crime he didn't commit.

     framed   robbed   stunned

7. A witness would _____ against him at the trial.
This witness would give information about the man's character.

     run   testify   sing

THE CASE
OF THE MILLION PESOS

Name _____

One way to summarize a story is to complete a report. Use the report below.

Detective's Report

Your Name: _____ Date: _____

Where did this crime take place? _____

What was the crime? _____

Who were the suspects? **What** was the evidence against each one?

Suspects	Evidence
1.	
2.	

How was the case solved? _____

_____

_____

••• THE CASE •••
OF THE MILLION PESOS

Name_____

A. Read the paragraph. Write *past, present,* or *future* above
each verb to show its tense.

Ms. Gomez just telephoned with bad news. Thieves removed

the new statue from the museum garden. She thinks Encyclopedia

will help us. I will call him in a few minutes. I certainly hope he

is at his house.

B. Finish each sentence by writing the past, the present, or
the future tense of the verb shown in parentheses.

1. Ms. Gomez _____ *(lock)* the museum gates at six o'clock every night.

2. Last night the statue _____ *(disappear)* from the garden.

3. The police _____ *(interview)* Ms. Gomez earlier this morning.

4. Tomorrow I _____ *(ask)* Encyclopedia for his ideas.

What do you think happened to the statue?
Write your ideas about the mystery.
Use at least two different verb tenses in your sentences.

_____

_____

SUMMARIZING
the **LEARNING** The _____ shows action that happens now

or that happens over and over. The _____ shows action that has

already happened. The _____ shows action that will happen.

THE CASE
OF THE MILLION PESOS

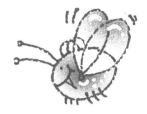

Name _____

Read each sentence below. Draw a line around the letter of
the correct definition for the underlined word. Then write a
sentence of your own, using the word in its other meaning.

1. After an evening baseball game, Encyclopedia solved his first
   international mystery.
   a. contest or sport of chance, skill, and/or endurance, with set rules
   b. animals or birds hunted for food or sport

   _____

2. Tim didn't catch a single fly during the game.
   a. small, winged insect
   b. baseball batted high over the field

   _____

3. Sally thought Tim might not be feeling well.
   a. in good health
   b. hole dug into the earth to reach oil, gas, or water

   _____

4. Tim's uncle had been accused of robbing a bank.
   a. land along the edge of a river or a stream
   b. place where money is lent, exchanged, and safeguarded

   _____

5. Sally said the real robber was bound to get caught.
   a. certain, sure
   b. tied or fastened, as with a band or a cord

   _____

THE CASE
OF THE MILLION PESOS

Name _____

Read each paragraph below. Then answer the questions that follow it.

1.   Encyclopedia has solved many mysteries before. When Tim's Uncle Duffy is accused of bank robbery, everyone turns to Encyclopedia for help.

a. What do you know about Encyclopedia's reputation?

_____

b. What evidence do you have?

_____

c. Imagine that you know someone like Encyclopedia in real life. What would you do if you were unfairly accused of a crime?

_____

_____

2.   Tim Gomez is usually a good baseball player. On one particular day, however, he strikes out six times in a row. In the outfield, he fails to catch any fly ball that comes near him.

a. What valid conclusion can you draw about how Tim feels?

_____

b. What evidence would you use to draw this conclusion?

_____

c. What real-life experiences would lead you to think that something is bothering Tim?

_____

_____

THE CASE
OF THE MILLION PESOS

Name _____

A. The underlined part of each sentence below is an example of figurative language. Rewrite each sentence, expressing the same idea without figurative language.

1. My legs are <u>falling off</u>.

_____

2. Something is <u>on his mind</u>.

_____

3. I played <u>like a cow on crutches</u>.

_____

4. Encyclopedia, Sally, and Benny <u>were bowled over</u> by the news.

_____

5. The police <u>threw him in jail</u> just the same.

_____

B. Use figurative language to complete each sentence.

1. Benny ran the bases like _____.

2. It got so dark that _____.

3. Encyclopedia was a _____.

4. Pedro Morales was _____.

124   *Figurative Language*   Practice Book ■ **EMERALD FOREST**

HBJ material copyrighted under notice appearing earlier in this work.

Name _____

Read the following story. Use clues in the story to figure out the meaning of each underlined word. Then write each word on the line next to its meaning.

Maria was <u>stunned</u> when Aunt Tanya opened the door. "Aunt Tanya," she cried, "you don't look well! What is the matter?"

Aunt Tanya said, "I guess I've got the same flu that many other people have now. I've been too weak even to work in my vegetable garden. Look at all the <u>shriveled</u> tomatoes on the vine." Maria said that she knew a woman in the village who could help. As Aunt Tanya <u>lumbered</u> up to her room, Maria remembered how quickly her aunt usually ran up the old wooden steps.

Maria reached the woman's house in the village and said <u>urgently</u>, "My aunt must have your help quickly." She then described her aunt's illness. The woman quickly <u>ransacked</u> a cupboard in her kitchen. "These are the <u>herbs</u> that will make your aunt well again," she said. She handed Maria two small jars filled with the dried leaves of special plants. Maria thanked her and ran out. She felt good knowing that Aunt Tanya would soon be working in her garden again.

1. _____ moved in a clumsy and heavy way

2. _____ wrinkled, dried up

3. _____ searched through every part of

4. _____ plants used as seasonings or medicine

5. _____ astonished or shocked

6. _____ in a demanding, serious way

• • • THE GOLD COIN • • •

Name _____

One way to summarize a story is to complete a story map.
Finish the one below by writing the answer in each empty box.

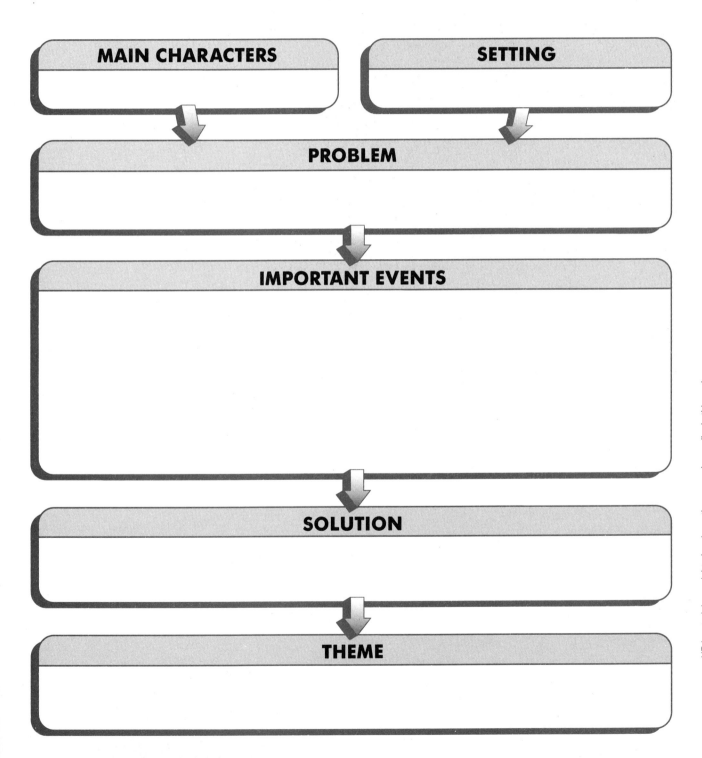

Name_____

A. Read the paragraph below. Underline each irregular verb. Circle the verbs that show past tense with helping verbs.

     For as long as anyone remembered, the thief had stolen everything that he wanted. He broke into people's homes and took their food as well as their money. He had thought only of himself. Now he looked at himself with their eyes, and he shuddered at what he saw.

B. Write the correct form of the verbs shown in parentheses to complete each sentence.

1. Everyone _____ *(say, said)* that the old woman was kind.

2. She _____ *(took, taken)* a gold coin to four different people.

3. The thief _____ *(saw, seen)* her walking down the path.

4. If he had _____ *(knew, known)* how kind she was, he might not have planned to rob her.

Write two sentences about Doña Josefa. Use the past tense of *go* and *think*.

_____

_____

SUMMARIZING *the* **L**EARNING   An irregular verb does not end with _____ in the past tense. Some irregular verbs show past tense by using a different form of the main verb with _____, _____, or _____.

Name _____

A. **Read each paragraph. Then draw a line around the letter in front of the sentence that best expresses a generalization based on the paragraph and on your own experience. Explain your choice.**

Angela spent a lot of time preparing for the exam. She went to the library every day for two weeks. While there, she read not only in her textbook, but she also looked up information in other books. She took notes, made outlines, and reviewed material.

a. Angela didn't enjoy studying.
b. Angela prepared well for the exam.
c. Angela is the best student in her class.

Explain your choice: _____

_____

Felipe got a bad cold in December. By January, he got rid of the cold, but then he fell down and hurt his ankle. Before his ankle healed, Felipe caught the chicken pox from his cousin Ramon. That kept him in bed for about ten days. At last, by late April, Felipe was starting to feel healthy again.

a. Ramon gave the chicken pox to Felipe.
b. Ramon is usually a healthy person.
c. Felipe didn't feel well for several months.

Explain your choice: _____

_____

Name _____

B. Read each paragraph. Write a generalization of your own based on the paragraph.

Fred was looking for an excuse to get rid of his old car, but he couldn't really find one. Each morning, he hoped the car wouldn't start when he put the key in. That beat-up old car just didn't seem to want to quit. Every morning, no matter how cold it was, the engine turned over, and the car made it to wherever Fred drove it. "Well," thought Fred, "maybe I'll just get a new paint job. Then I might feel better about driving this old car around town."

Generalization: _____

_____

By the age of six months, babies can lift up their heads and chests. They can also sit up with support. By nine months, babies try to crawl. They can sit up without support, and they can pull themselves up to a standing position. By their first birthday, they can crawl on hands and knees and walk around furniture while holding on. Some babies can walk alone.

Generalization: _____

_____

• • • • THE GOLD COIN • • • •

Name _____

Each sentence below is taken from the story. Read each one.
On the line provided, write *character*, *setting*, or *plot* to tell
which story element is demonstrated. Explain your answer.

1. Juan had been a thief for many years. _____

_____

2. Juan decided instantly that all the woman's gold must be his.

_____

3. The countryside had been deserted, but here, along the

riverbank, were two huts. _____

_____

4. But he quickly grew impatient. _____

_____

5. Juan had forgotten the taste of a home-cooked meal and the

pleasure that comes from sharing it with others. _____

_____

6. By the light of the moon, father and son guided their boat

across the river. _____

7. "Over to the other side of the mountain," the young man
replied, pointing to the vague outline of mountains in the

night sky. _____

8. So Juan spent the next day in the fields, bathed in sweat

from sunup to sundown. _____

Name _____

A. Read the information in the chart. Using the definitions, answer each question below.

Prefix	Meaning	Suffix	Meaning
de- *im-*	"to remove" "not"	*-ly* *-less* *-er*	"in the manner of" "without" "one who"; "more"

1. The Latin root *sperare* means "to hope." What do you think

the English word *despair* means? _____

2. The word *patient* means "calm and understanding." How

would you describe someone who is not patient? _____

3. The word *speech* means "the act of speaking." If someone
could not speak for a time, what word would describe the

person? _____

4. The word *amiable* is from a Latin word meaning "friend." If

someone acts amiably, how does he or she act? _____

5. A farmer is one who farms. A teacher is one who teaches.

What would you call one who heals? _____

B. Use the base words below and the prefixes and suffixes in
the chart to form words. Then write a sentence using each
of the words you formed.

1. anxious _____

2. possible _____

••• A River Ran Wild •••

Name _____

Answer each question, writing one letter on each blank. Use each word in the box once. Then unscramble the letters in the squares to answer the riddle at the bottom.

> conquer   current   chemicals
> decades   descendant   native

1. What do you call a person who was born in a certain place?

_ _ _ □ _ _

2. What is the part of a stream that flows?

_ _ _ □ _ □ _

3. Which word means "periods of ten years"?

_ _ _ _ _ □ _

4. What do you call substances such as sulphur and phosphorus?

_ _ _ _ _ _ _ □ _

5. What is another word meaning "child" or "grandchild"?

_ _ □ _ _ _ _ _ _ _

6. Which word means "defeat by force"?

_ _ _ _ _ _ □

WHAT DOES A RIVER DO IN THE RIVERBED?

___ ___   ___ ___ ___ ___ **P** ___

Make up your own Secret Agent code. Choose a number or a symbol to stand for each letter of the alphabet. Then write the words from the box in your code. Challenge your partner to crack the code!

HBJ material copyrighted under notice appearing earlier in this work.

Name_____

A. Complete the summary map below to help you
remember the main ideas in "A River Ran Wild."

Topic:	The Nashua River
Setting:	

Main Idea 1:	Chief Weeawa and his people settle by the river.
Important Detail:	

Main Idea 2:	
Important Detail:	

Main Idea 3:	
Important Detail:	

Main Idea 4:	
Important Detail:	

B. Write a brief summary of the selection.

_____

_____

_____

••• A RIVER RAN WILD •••

Name_____

In addition to rivers, there are many different kinds of bodies of water. Look at the picture. It shows some natural bodies of water that can be found throughout the United States. Read the numbered clues. Then write the correct number next to each word on the picture.

___ ocean

___ bay

___ lake

___ tributary

___ gulf

___ stream

___ swamp

1. a large body of salt water

2. a small area of ocean partly surrounded by land

3. a large area of ocean partly surrounded by land

4. a body of fresh or salt water surrounded by land

5. a small body of running water

6. a small river that flows into a larger one

7. low, wet land

Working with a partner, make a list of the bodies of water that you find near the following cities: New Orleans, Pittsburgh, Atlanta, San Francisco, Milwaukee, and Boston. Use an atlas of the United States to locate the cities. Share your list with your classmates.

••• A RIVER RAN WILD •••

Name_____

A. Read the paragraph below. Underline each adverb.
Draw an arrow to the verb that it describes.

The trader came to the trading post early. He took an

armload of firewood indoors. Then he patiently built a fire

in the old iron stove. Sometimes the stove smoked, and

soot covered everything. The wood slowly caught

fire, and the old stove glowed cheerfully.

B. Complete each sentence with an adverb. Your adverb
should answer the question in parentheses.

She leaves for school _____. *(When?)*

Her dog trots _____ down the street after her. *(How?)*

When the dog hears her whistle, it runs _____. *(Where?)*

Write one sentence about your own pet or someone
else's pet. Use an adverb in the sentence.

_____

_____

SUMMARIZING
the **L**EARNING   An adverb describes a _____. Most adverbs tell

_____, _____, or _____ an action takes place.

Name_____

This letter was written by a young English settler to a friend back home. Rewrite a briefer message on the smaller piece of paper. Be sure to include the same information.

Dear Jeffrey,
   We arrived here in the New World in the spring. The Nashua is really beautiful. There are cattails along the riverbanks, and the Indians use them to thatch their dwellings. They plant corn and squash for eating. They use wood from the forest to make arrows for hunting and canoes for traveling.
   I made friends with an Indian girl about my age. She told me that the river, land, and forest provide everything her people need.

                    Write soon. I miss you.

                              Your friend,

                                 Amy

Dear Jeffrey,

                              Your friend,
                              Amy

••• A RIVER RAN WILD •••

Name_____

Years later, Amy's daughter wrote a letter to a friend. The
Nashua River had changed, and so had the lives of many
children.

Dear Phoebe,
  I just got a job at a factory. It overlooks the Nashua
River, but we keep our windows closed because the river
smells bad. My job is to weave thread into cloth. In
another part of the factory, other workers dye the cloth
beautiful colors. Last week, they were using red dyes.
The river was red for the whole week as they dumped the
old dyes into the water. The week before, they were using
blue dyes. Guess what color the water was then!
  My mom told me that the river used to be clear. She
says there used to be a lot of fish in it, and lots of
animals came to its banks. It's hard to believe. I wonder
if it will ever be clean again.
                                        Your friend,
                                        Alice

What if Alice had just a postcard to write on? Write what
she might have put on a postcard, and make sure you tell
Phoebe the same information.

Dear Phoebe,

                                        Your friend,
                                        Alice

••• A RIVER RAN WILD •••

Name_____

Read each situation below. Then write a sentence that tells what might have caused it. Write another sentence that tells what might be an effect of it.

1. Indians and wildlife live together in harmony in the river valley.

> Possible cause:

> Possible effect:

2. An industrial revolution brings many factories to the banks of the river.

> Possible cause:

> Possible effect:

3. People protest against the polluting of the river.

> Possible cause:

> Possible effect:

Name _____

Write a sentence that tells what is happening or might be happening in each picture. In each sentence, use the word given below the picture.

dugout

contradicting

1. _____

_____

_____

2. _____

_____

_____

yoked

attentive

3. _____

_____

_____

4. _____

_____

_____

••• ON THE BANKS OF PLUM CREEK •••

Name _____

A. One way to summarize a story is to complete a chart like
the one below. Use the chart before and after reading.

Prior knowledge about living on a prairie farm in the 1870s	What was learned about living on a prairie farm in the 1870s

B. Use your chart to write a brief summary statement about
life on the prairie in the 1870s.

_____

_____

_____

••• ON THE BANKS OF PLUM CREEK •••

Name_____

If you could go back in time to the days of Laura Ingalls Wilder's childhood, you would probably see some items you might not recognize. Label each picture with a word from the box. The sentences will give you clues.

diligence	keelboat	bandbox
sampler	bellows	tintype

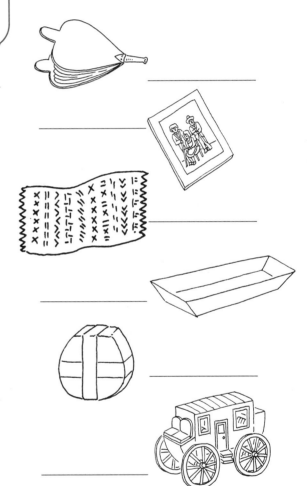

Pioneers used *bellows* made of wood, leather, and metal to pump air to help start a fire.

Road travel was difficult in a *diligence,* or coach.

Settlers traveling on rivers might build a flat-bottomed *keelboat* to carry their belongings.

Many pioneer families had a *tintype,* or photograph printed on thin metal, of a relative.

A woman might have stored a hat in a rounded *bandbox.*

A girl could show off her sewing skill by displaying a *sampler* she had embroidered with a fancy design.

With a group of classmates or a partner, make a mural or a poster showing a scene from the old West. Label items that might not be familiar to many people today.

Name_____

A. Read the sentences. Underline the adverbs that show comparison. Also underline any word that helps an adverb make a comparison.

This was the longest Pa had ever been away. Of the three girls, Mary waited the most patiently for his return. At noon, Laura heard the dog bark. Jack barked longer than usual. Laura could run more quickly than Mary, so she reached the door first .

B. Add *-er, -est, more,* or *most* to the adverb in parentheses to complete each sentence.

Pa yelled _____ than he had ever yelled before. *(loud)*

Pete headed back to the barn _____ than Bright did. *(willingly)*

All three children were upset, but Carrie took the _____ to calm down. *(long)*

Write a sentence or two comparing how people traveled during Laura's childhood to how people travel today. Use adverbs in your sentences.

_____

_____

SUMMARIZING
the **L**EARNING   Add _____ to short adverbs to compare two

actions. Add _____ to short adverbs to compare three or more actions.

Use _____ and _____ before adverbs that have two

or more syllables.

••• ON THE BANKS OF PLUM CREEK •••

Name_____

When Pa goes to town, he always buys presents for his children. He wants to tell the children about the store where he buys the presents. Read what Pa is thinking. Then rewrite his thoughts in your own words.

The store in town is an amazing place. They have all sorts of things for people to buy. There is a section of the store that has flour, sugar, salt, and other baking supplies. They also have lots of interesting spices and herbs, such as cinnamon, pepper, thyme, and oregano. There is a fabric section, where Ma buys calico and thread to make new dresses. The candy section has several barrels full of treats for my children. The candy I chose this time is called hoarhound candy. It's the color of maple sugar, and the inside of it is hard, clear, and dark brown.

ACTIVITY CORNER

With a partner, choose three articles from a newspaper. Paraphrase a paragraph from each article. Write titles for your new paragraphs.

••• ON THE BANKS OF PLUM CREEK •••

Name_____

Read the sentences below. Then write what the sentences tell you about each character's mood, feelings, or personality.

1. Without thinking about his own safety, Pa ran after the runaway oxen. Although he could have been hurt, Pa kept trying to get the oxen to swerve. He had to save his family.

1. The sentences tell me that Pa is

_____

_____.

2. Because she was shaking so hard, Ma had a hard time getting out of the cart. Her face was drained of all its color.

2. The sentences tell me that Ma is

_____

_____.

3. Carrie couldn't stop crying. She stood close to her mother as she continued to sob for several minutes.

3. The sentences tell me that Carrie is

_____

_____.

4. Laura jumped up on Pa's knee and looked at him as if she expected a treat. Her eyes were shining.

4. The sentences tell me that Laura is

_____

_____.

Put on a skit with a partner. Demonstrate qualities or feelings, such as generosity, athletic ability, cheerfulness, thoughtfulness, sorrow, joy, or anger. Ask other classmates what they can tell about the characters in your skit, based on what the characters do.

••• ON THE BANKS OF PLUM CREEK •••

Name_____

A. Study the map below, and answer the questions that follow.

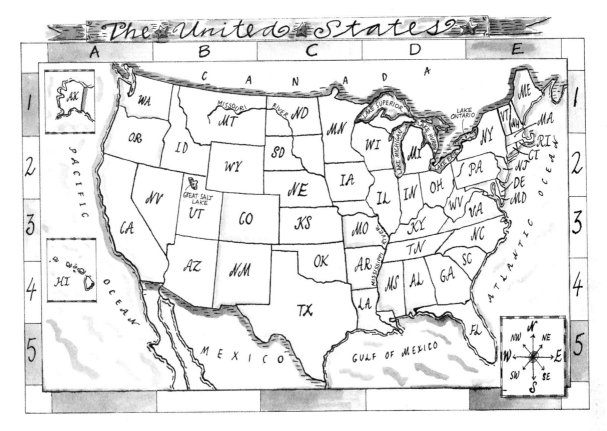

1. Laura Ingalls Wilder was born in Wisconsin in 1867. If you were in Mississippi, in which direction would you travel to get to Wisconsin? _____

2. Laura's family moved from Wisconsin to Kansas. In which direction did they travel?

_____

3. Later, they moved from Kansas back to Wisconsin. Name two different routes they might have taken.

   a. _____

   b. _____

HBJ material copyrighted under notice appearing earlier in this work.

➡

Name_____

4. Imagine that Laura's family moved from Wisconsin to the larger part of Michigan. If they went the shortest way, which body of water would they have to cross?

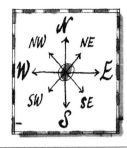

_____

If they wanted to avoid crossing this body of water, through which states would they have to travel?

_____

B. Now use the letters across the top and the numbers along the sides of the map to help you with numbers 5 through 7.

5. Name a state located in area C-3.

_____

6. If you wanted to get from area A-1 to area C-3, which states might you travel through?

_____

7. What is the letter and number of your city or area?

_____

Find a map of your city or area. Get together with several classmates and mark routes you take to get home, to go to a park, to go to the library, and so on. You may want to use colored markers. Take turns explaining the routes you marked, using phrases like *go west* or *turn right*.

••• NO STAR NIGHTS •••

Name_____

The guide has forgotten some of the words she needs to lead visitors on a tour of the factory. Help her by writing each word where it belongs.

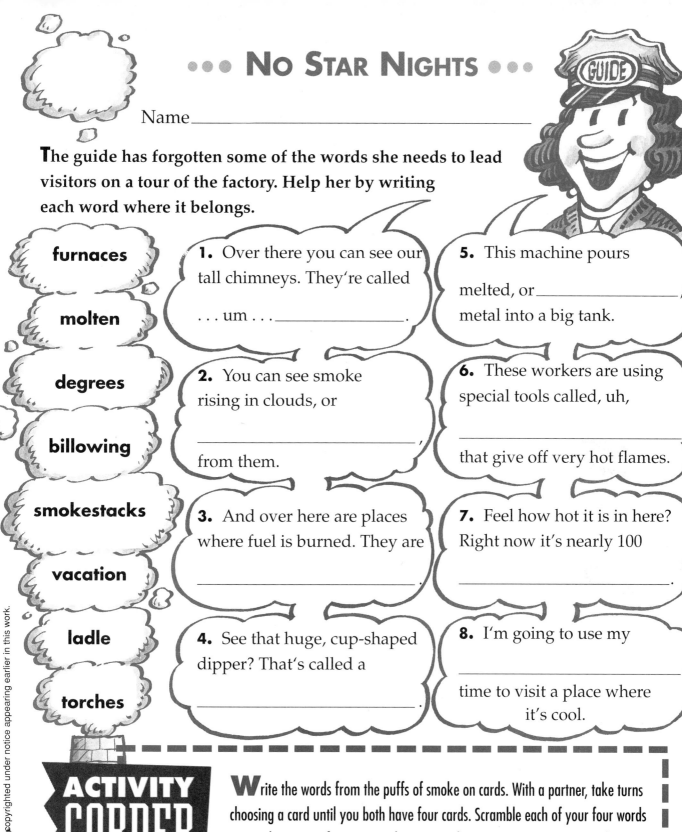

furnaces

molten

degrees

billowing

smokestacks

vacation

ladle

torches

1. Over there you can see our tall chimneys. They're called . . . um . . . _____.

2. You can see smoke rising in clouds, or _____, from them.

3. And over here are places where fuel is burned. They are _____.

4. See that huge, cup-shaped dipper? That's called a _____.

5. This machine pours melted, or _____, metal into a big tank.

6. These workers are using special tools called, uh, _____ that give off very hot flames.

7. Feel how hot it is in here? Right now it's nearly 100 _____.

8. I'm going to use my _____ time to visit a place where it's cool.

ACTIVITY CORNER

Write the words from the puffs of smoke on cards. With a partner, take turns choosing a card until you both have four cards. Scramble each of your four words on another piece of paper. Switch papers with your partner. Race to see who can unscramble all four of each other's words the fastest.

RENFRO

Name_____

A. Complete the chart below to show how the steel mill was important to the town in "No Star Nights."

Main Idea:	The mill affected the way the whole town looked.
Detail:	
Detail:	

Main Idea:	The mill influenced how families lived.
Detail:	
Detail:	

Main Idea:	The mill even affected children at school.
Detail:	
Detail:	

B. Write a brief summary statement about the selection.

_____

••• No Star Nights •••

Name_____

A. **Read the paragraph and underline each negative.**

Samsonville isn't a very exciting place. There is nowhere for kids to go on weekends. Nobody goes downtown after dinner. None of the stores are open after 6:00 P.M. My friends and I have never found a good place to get together and talk.

B. **Answer each question using a negative. Write complete sentences.**

Do you ever go roller-skating at night?

_____

Does anyone in your town teach roller-skating?

_____

Is there anywhere to roller-skate in town?

_____

Write a few sentences about a town. Use at least two negatives.

_____

_____

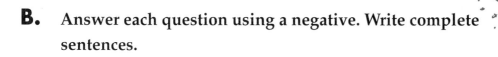

SUMMARIZING *the* **L**EARNING   A negative means _____. Some common negative words

include _____ and _____. In the

contraction *isn't*, the combination *n't* stands for _____.

HBJ material copyrighted under notice appearing earlier in this work.

••• No Star Nights •••

Name_____

Mr. Olsen works different shifts at the mill. Sometimes he works days, and sometimes he works nights. Refer to his schedule to answer the questions below.

WORK SCHEDULE

Month	Days On	Hours	Days Off
January	Mon.–Fri.	3 p.m.–11 p.m.	Sat., Sun.
February	Tues.–Sat.	11 p.m.–7 a.m.	Sun., Mon.
March	Mon.–Tues.; Thurs.–Sat.	7 a.m.–3 p.m.	Wed., Sun.

1. When Mr. Olsen works, how many hours a day does he work? _____

2. What is the one day Mr. Olsen always gets off? _____

3. Mr. Olsen is usually asleep within four hours after getting off work. By what time does he go to sleep during January? _____

4. During which month does Mr. Olsen not get two days in a row off? _____

5. Which month's schedule would you like best? Explain why.

_____

_____

Make a weekly schedule of your own. Compare it with a partner's schedule. Discuss ways you could change your schedule to allow for more time to do what you want to do.

••• NO STAR NIGHTS •••

Name_____

Josephine likes to talk a lot. Joe likes to use few words.
Write Joe's half of this conversation by summarizing what
Josephine has just said.

My dad and everyone else's dad worked in the mill.
Each man carried a tin lunchbox with at least two
sandwiches, two pieces of fruit, and something for
dessert, like a piece of pie. Each one also carried a big
metal thermos bottle filled with something hot to drink.

So what you're saying is this:

All of us kids liked it best when Dad had some daylight
hours to spend with us. We would play baseball until
the sun went down and it got too dark. I'd be the
catcher, and my brother would be the outfielder. Dad
would usually pitch, and we'd have a great time.

So what you're saying is this:

One time I got a piece of graphite in my eye. It
really hurt, and I couldn't get it out, no matter what I
did. When Mom took me to the doctor, I was afraid.
But anything was better than having that piece of
graphite stuck in my eye.

So what you're saying is this:

Name_____

Think about the people in the town in
"No Star Nights." Then read the words below.
Who might have said them? Explain your
reasons for drawing your conclusions.

Can you imagine
what would have happened if
we had dumped this slag? It
would have been very
dangerous for those girls.

Who might have said this?

_____

Reasons: _____

_____

I'm glad I practiced. I'd
hate to drop this thing in
front of all these people.

Who might have said this?

_____

Reasons: _____

_____

I thought this day would
never end. It was so hot
at work I thought I'd
collapse.

Who might have said this?

_____

Reasons: _____

_____

ACTIVITY CORNER

With a partner, look through a magazine with many pictures. Study about ten of
the pictures closely, without looking at any nearby words. Discuss the conclusions you
could draw about what is happening in the pictures. Write captions, or sentences
telling what the pictures are about.

• • • TOTEM POLE • • •

Name _____

Read each sentence below. Draw a line under the correct meaning of the word in dark print in each sentence.

1. Some Native Americans of the Northwest are not able to follow the **traditions** of their great-grandparents.
   a. customs or beliefs passed on from generation to generation
   b. political beliefs of a country
   c. ways of conducting scientific experiments

2. Native Americans who live on a **reservation** usually have a strong tribal identity.
   a. broad stretch of land covered with trees
   b. land set aside by the government for a special purpose
   c. abandoned park

3. When a chief erected a totem pole, a **ceremony** was held to honor the chief's ancestors.
   a. act performed on special occasions
   b. task or chore done every day
   c. contest to determine athletic skill

4. The artist used **charcoal** to draw the figures on the totem pole before carving them out.
   a. a carving tool
   b. a wedge-shaped piece of metal
   c. black substance made by burning wood

5. Sometimes the chief of a **clan** invited many people to an enormous feast.
   a. union of states or countries
   b. group of related families
   c. company that makes and sells a product

6. Native Americans of the Northwest considered copper a **precious** metal and often gave articles made of it as gifts.
   a. highly valued   **b.** ordinary   **c.** not worth much

••• TOTEM POLE •••

Name _____

A. Use the chart to summarize the selection.

MAIN IDEA	MAIN IDEA	MAIN IDEA
Detail	Detail	Detail
Detail	Detail	Detail
Detail	Detail	Detail

B. On another sheet of paper, write a brief summary statement about the selection.

••• TOTEM POLE •••

Name_____

A. Read the sentences. Underline each incorrect word.
Write the correct word on the line.

My grandmother is a very good potter. Her pots are

beautiful. Their _____ on display at the museum.

My too _____ older sisters are learning from her,

but there _____ pots don't come out as well as

hers. My grandmother says that each pot has it's _____

own story.

B. Choose the correct word from the words in parentheses.
Write the word on the line.

Have you ever put _____ *(your, you're)* fingers into wet clay?

_____ *(Its, It's)* fun to make clay pots.

My uncle is a potter, _____ *(to, two, too)*.

That pot right _____ *(their, they're, there)* is one that I made.

Write two sentences about your own or someone else's
pet. Use one of the words in parentheses above in each sentence.

_____

_____

SUMMARIZING
the **L**EARNING   Two words that sound like *two* are _____ and _____.

The word *good* describes a _____. The word *well* describes a _____.

Use _____ to mean "in that place." Use _____ to mean "it is."

HBJ material copyrighted under notice appearing earlier in this work.

• • • TOTEM POLE • • •

Name _____

On the line, write *fact* or *opinion* to describe each sentence below.
Draw a line around words that signal an opinion.

1. Totem poles are found only in northwestern North America. _____

2. European explorers first reported seeing totem poles in

Alaska in the late 1700s. _____

3. I believe totem poles are the most beautiful form of art ever

found in northwestern North America. _____

4. Because no attempt is made to preserve them, totem poles

last only about fifty or sixty years. _____

5. I think totem poles are beautiful works of art that should be preserved.

_____

6. Totem poles usually last for one lifetime. _____

7. Totem-pole carvers are the most talented people in their tribe. _____

8. It requires a certain amount of skill to carve a totem pole. _____

9. Twelve totem poles were displayed at the Chicago World's

Fair in 1893. _____

10. I feel that people who carve their own initials on totem poles

should be arrested for vandalism. _____

• •

SUMMARIZING
the **L**EARNING   I know that a statement is a fact if _____

_____. I know that a statement is an opinion

if _____. ⇨

••• TOTEM POLE •••

Name_____

Read the facts and opinions. Fill in the empty speech balloons with a fact or an opinion on the same topic.

FACTS

OPINIONS

Kingston is a small town in Washington State.

The Tsimshian language is easy to learn.

In some Indian legends, Raven is a trickster.

Totem poles are the best art in the world.

The old way of raising a totem pole is better than the new way.

With a partner, choose an editorial from a newspaper. Identify the facts in the editorial. Then identify the opinions.

• • • TOTEM POLE • • •

Name _____

Read the paragraphs on this page. Then, on the next page, make an outline of the information they contain.

The Indians of the Northwest Coast made several kinds of totem poles. House pillars, probably the earliest type of totem pole ever made, were supports for heavy beams. Sometimes, carvings were made directly on the pillar. At other times, a false house pillar was constructed. Carvings were made on another piece of red cedar and then attached to the pillar. Removing this false front made it easy to save the carvings in case of flood, fire, or moving.

The memorial pole, honoring a chief who had died, was considered the most important kind of totem pole. The new chief would have the memorial pole carved and put up, but only after having ruled for a year.

The heraldic portal, or family pole, was placed in front of a home. A large opening near the pole's bottom allowed entrance to the home. Carvings on the pole told of the importance of the family living there.

The welcoming pole was used by people who lived on a waterfront. Usually found in pairs, these poles marked off land on the shore to show possession.

Finally, the shame pole was used to force payment of debts. The debtor's totem was carved upside down. When the story of the unpaid debt was shown in public, the debtor was usually shamed into paying right away.

• • • TOTEM POLE • • •

Name _____

I. _____

   A. _____

   B. _____

   C. _____

II. _____

   A. _____

   B. _____

III. _____

   A. _____

   B. _____

   C. _____

IV. _____

   A. _____

   B. _____

      1. _____

      2. _____

V. _____

   A. _____

   B. _____

••• JUST A DREAM •••

Name_____

Help Daniel tell about his scary dream! Fill in the missing
words. The words you will need are hiding under the bed.

What a dream! It seemed to take place about a hundred years from now.

Just like on a _____ school day, I was waiting for the bus.

Suddenly three of my friends ran toward me, _____, "A

dinosaur is coming!" "No way!" I said. "Dinosaurs lived in the past, not

the _____ !" Was I ever wrong! A huge cloud of dust came

billowing up the street. We _____ through the _____,

and there was an enormous *Tyrannosaurus rex!* It thundered up to us,

stopped, and asked politely, "Pardon me, but may I get a drink from that

fire _____?"

haze	**future**	**shrieking**
usual	**peered**	**hydrant**

Working with a partner, make a crossword puzzle using the words under
Daniel's bed. Use a dictionary to help you write the clues. Then challenge a
classmate to solve your puzzle!

Name_____

A. One way to summarize a story is to make a cause-and-effect chart. Complete the chart below.

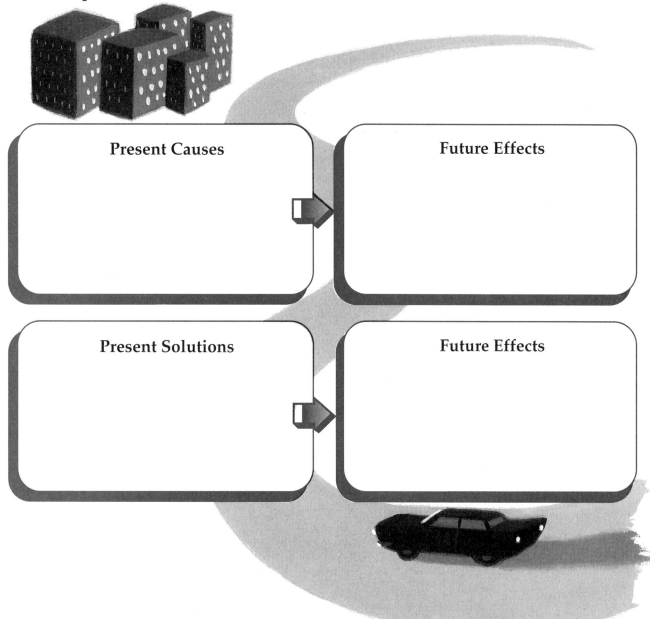

Present Causes	Future Effects

Present Solutions	Future Effects

B. Use the information in your cause-and-effect chart to write a brief summary statement about the selection.

_____

_____

••• JUST A DREAM •••

Name_____

A. Read the paragraph below. Draw a box around each separate item in a series.

What inventions will the future bring? One hundred years ago, no one had heard of laser beams, space shuttles, or microwave ovens. Perhaps in the future, people will ride in floating cars, eat special foods, and live for two hundred years. To picture the future, you must be imaginative, open-minded, and curious.

B. Rewrite each sentence below. Add commas between items in a series.

Perhaps newspapers magazines and books will be electronic.

_____

_____

Will schools be smaller larger or the same size?

_____

_____

I think more people will eat well take vitamins and get plenty of exercise.

_____

_____

SUMMARIZING **t h e L**EARNING   To punctuate items in a series, put _____ after

each item except _____.

••• JUST A DREAM •••

Name_____

A. **S**ort these sentences by writing their numbers on the correct trash can.

1. The valleys were filled with smog, and so was the Grand Canyon.

2. The woodcutters thought toothpicks were more important than trees. Walter, on the other hand, thought trees were more important than toothpicks.

3. Fishermen usually throw small fish back, but in Walter's dream they kept them.

4. Rose was happy with her birthday present, but Walter thought it was stupid.

5. Walter liked jelly doughnuts, and he also liked television.

6. Rose received a tree for her birthday, and so did Walter.

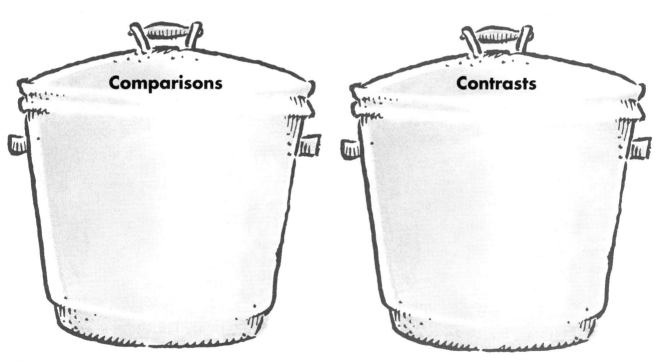

Comparisons   Contrasts

B. Write a sentence of your own, contrasting the "old" Walter with the "new" Walter.

_____

_____

HBJ material copyrighted under notice appearing earlier in this work.

••• JUST A DREAM •••

Name_____

The prefix *in-* means "into."

The Latin root *inflatus* means "to blow."

The suffix *-able* means "can do" or "can be done."

The Greek root *hydro* means "water."

The prefix *de-* means "to remove."

The Greek root *tele* means "from afar."

The Latin root *vision* means "sight" or "something seen."

The prefix *re-* means "to do something again."

The root *planer* means "fly" or "skim."

The Latin root *port* means "carry."

Based on Walter's dreams, what do you think these words mean? Write each meaning, and then use the word in a sentence.

1. hydroplane _____

_____

2. dehydrate _____

_____

3. teleport _____

_____

4. inflatable _____

_____

5. revision _____

_____

Name_____

Use what you know about the new, improved Walter to predict what he would say next. Write his words, and then explain your prediction.

1.

 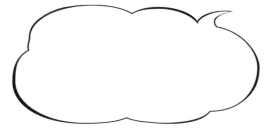 

Walter would say this because _____.

2.

Walter would say this because _____.

3.

Walter would say this because _____.

ACTIVITY CORNER

Walter changed during this story. Will he continue to change during the coming year? With a group, discuss possibilities for Walter's future. Then create a group mural that shows what Walter's next birthday might be like.

••• A RIVER DREAM •••

Name_____

Use the clues to decide which word to write on each fish.
Use each word in the boat once.

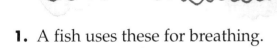

trout   hovering   cast
reel   weight   gills   exclaimed

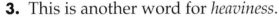

1. A fish uses these for breathing.

2. A _____ is the throw of a fishing line or net.

3. This is another word for *heaviness*.

4. When an insect stays in one place in the air, it is doing this.

5. This is a type of fish.

6. You might use this spool for winding your fishing line.

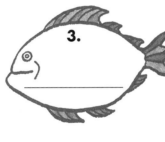

7. If you have caught a big fish, you might have _____, "Wow! Look at this one!"

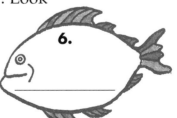

ACTIVITY CORNER

Make a picture dictionary with a small group of classmates. At the bottom of each page, write one of the words from the boat. Draw a picture that illustrates the word's meaning. Then bind your dictionary and decorate its cover. Share your dictionary with younger students.

••• A RIVER DREAM •••

Name_____

A. One way to summarize a story is to complete a prediction chart. Finish the chart below to show what you predicted and what actually happened in "A River Dream."

	What I Predict	**What Happens**
Think about the main character.		
Think about the title.		
Think about the ending.		

B. Use the information in your chart to write a brief summary of the story.

_____

_____

_____

••• A RIVER DREAM •••

Name_____

A. Read the dialogue. Underline the word in each sentence that is set apart by a comma.

"Jennie, is there anywhere to rent a boat around here?"

"No, I don't think so. Well, wait a minute. Yes, there is one small lake. Do you know where Highlands Park is, Erin?"

B. Rewrite each sentence. Add commas where they belong.

Yes there are still a few boats left at the dock.

_____

Well you certainly won't win any prizes for your rowing!

_____

Do you want to rest for a while Daniel?

_____

Write a brief conversation that takes place between two friends at a lake. Use an introductory word in at least one sentence, and use direct address in another.

_____

_____

SUMMARIZING *the* **L**EARNING Use a comma to set off the words _____, _____,

or _____ at the beginning of a sentence. Use a comma to set off the

_____ of someone who is being spoken to directly in a sentence.

... A RIVER DREAM ...

Name_____

The trout have suggestions for improving these sentences.
Rewrite the second sentence in each pair below. Use the trouts'
suggestions instead of the underlined words or phrases.

1. Mark had been sick for several days. <u>Mark</u> had a high fever.

_____

2. Mark saw a rowboat. He thought to <u>Mark</u>, "I'll borrow it."

_____

3. Mark saw a man on the riverbank. He waved to <u>the man</u>.

_____

4. Uncle Scott caught a trout. <u>The trout</u> had a hook in its mouth.

_____

5. Mark let it go. The trout shook <u>the trout</u> before swimming
away.

_____

6. Mark's mother came into his room. <u>Mark's mother</u> said,"I
think his fever is going down."

_____

them   him   itself   she   it   they   he   her

herself   himself   themselves

With a partner, find an article about fish in a magazine or an encyclopedia. Identify each pronoun and the word it stands for.

••• A RIVER DREAM •••

Name_____

Each of these paragraphs has to fit into one of the empty spaces in the tackle box below. They won't fit unless they're a lot shorter. Use just one sentence to summarize each paragraph. Write the summaries in the tackle box.

1. The beautiful trout put up a strong fight. It tried to get away, leaping and twisting in the river. No matter what it did, it could not break Mark's fishing line. After a long fight, the trout finally got tired, and Mark was able to reel it in.

2. Mark admired the fish for a few minutes. It was a magnificent trout. Never before had Mark seen one that was so beautiful. He could really understand why it was called a "rainbow trout."

• • • A RIVER DREAM • • •

Name _____

A. Use the information in the charts to answer the questions below.

Prefix	Meaning
pro-	"in front of"
inter-	"between"
com-,	"with"
con-	
pre-	"before"

Suffix	Meaning
-tion	"state or quality of"
-ate	"state or quality of"

1. The Latin root *clamare* means "to cry out." What do you

think the English word *proclaim* means? _____

2. The Latin root *parare* means "to get" or "to obtain." What do

you think the English word *preparation* means? _____

_____

3. The Latin root *fortis* means "strength." What do you think

the English word *comfort* means? _____

4. The Latin root *rumpere* means "to break." What do you think

the English word *interrupt* means? _____

5. The Latin root *sider* means "star." Long ago, people looked
to the stars above for an answer as they thought about an
everyday problem. What do you think the English word

considerate means? _____

B. On a separate sheet of paper, use each of these words in a
sentence: *proclaim, preparation, comfort, interrupt,
considerate.*

••• Mufaro's Beautiful Daughters •••

Name _____

Use clues in the story to figure out the meaning of each underlined word. Then write each word on the line next to its meaning.

Many years ago, a king needed to decide which of two noblemen he could trust. He summoned them to his castle to test them, and as they approached, the dark outline of the castle was silhouetted against the moonlit sky.

The king showed the noblemen a set of laws that would have treated his subjects harshly. "Noblemen," the king said, "please advise me about these laws. What will my subjects think of them?"

"Your Highness," the first nobleman said, "all your subjects will praise you if you issue these laws. These measures prove your bountiful kindness."

"Your Highness," the second nobleman said, "if you are not considerate of your subjects' needs, how can you expect them to be loyal to you?" The second nobleman gave his opinion honestly, with no fear of the king's temper.

After both had spoken, the king said, "The man I can trust is the one who acknowledges the truth." He banished the first nobleman to a faraway land and invited the second nobleman to live in his castle as his highest adviser.

1. _____ notices or recognizes

2. _____ frame of mind, mood

3. _____ thoughtful

4. _____ express approval of

5. _____ give advice or an opinion

6. _____ plentiful, more than enough

7. _____ outlined against a light background

• • • MUFARO'S BEAUTIFUL DAUGHTERS • • •

Name _____

Finish the story frame below by completing each
sentence.

This story takes place
First we meet two sisters,
Nyasha is
Manyara is
One day the king announces
After that, Manyara leaves
Along the way, Manyara is unkind to
On her journey, Nyasha treats everyone she meets with
At the gate of the city Manyara is terrified because
Nyasha goes to face the monster and finds
Manyara becomes

Write a brief summary statement about the story.

_____

_____

_____

MUFARO'S BEAUTIFUL DAUGHTERS

Name _____

A. On each line, write an adjective that could be added
to the sentence.

1. One day, Nyasha noticed a small garden snake resting

beneath a _____ yam vine.

2. Nyoka spent many days in the _____ garden
while Nyasha tended it.

3. The Great King chose a _____ messenger to
spread a message throughout the kingdom.

4. The Great King wanted a _____ wife.

5. A _____ boy asked Manyara for some food.

6. "Tomorrow I will become your _____ queen."

B. Write a sentence about each of the following characters
and objects. Use at least three adjectives in each sentence,
and circle them.

1. Mufaro: _____

_____

_____

2. Nyoka: _____

_____

_____

3. yams: _____

_____

_____

Name_____

A. **Read the paragraphs below. Find and underline the direct quotations in them.**

> The queen raised her hand for silence. "My loyal subjects," she began,
> "I have looked high and low for a new king. Finally, I have found him."
> The queen introduced the new king and the crowd cheered.
>
> "Thank you for your kind welcome," said the new king. "I will try to serve
> you well."

B. **Add quotation marks to the sentences below.**

The prince asked,   How can I help you?
For starters, you can get this thorn out of my foot,   said the lion.
That should be easy,   answered the prince.
Is there something else I can do?   he asked.
The lion smiled and said,   I would like to borrow your hat.

On the line below, write what you think the prince will say
next to the lion. Use quotation marks in your sentence.

_____

SUMMARIZING
the **L**EARNING   The exact words someone says are called a

_____. _____ are placed before and after a

direct quotation to set it off from the rest of a sentence.

••• MUFARO'S BEAUTIFUL DAUGHTERS •••

Name_____

Read the sentences below, and think about the author's use of vivid language. Underline some of the words and phrases that help you picture the scene in your mind.

> Thick, fluffy mist covered the valley floor like a quilt. In the far distance, Queen Nyasha's palace rose through the mist and sparkled like pure gold in the light.

Rewrite each sentence below using vivid, descriptive language. Try to help the reader feel as if he or she is really there.

1. Nyasha saw a flower.

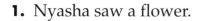

2. The flower smelled nice.

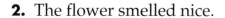

3. The castle was beautiful.

_____

4. The birds sang.

_____

5. Nyasha felt the wind.

_____

Write a description of the most beautiful outdoor scene you can imagine. Trade papers with a partner, and draw what your partner has described.

• • • Mufaro's Beautiful Daughters • • •

Name _____

Read the paragraph below. Draw a line around the word that gives a clue that two elements are being compared. Underline each word or phrase that gives a clue that two elements are being contrasted. Then answer the questions that follow.

> **M**anyara was a beautiful young woman, and her sister Nyasha was beautiful, too. Their personalities, however, were quite different from each other. Manyara was almost always in a bad mood. Her sister, on the other hand, was usually in a good mood. Manyara was always mean to her sister, but Nyasha was always kind.

1. What is alike about the two sisters? _____

2. What is different about them? _____

_____

_____

• •

SUMMARIZING *the* **L**EARNING

1. As I read, I compare in order to identify how two things are _____. Sometimes a writer uses a signal word or phrase, such as _____

_____, to show a comparison.

2. When I read, I contrast in order to identify how two things are _____. Sometimes a writer uses a signal word or phrase, such as _____

_____, to show a contrast.

Name_____

Help Queen Nyasha remodel her courtyard. First, read the directions all the way through once. Then, as you follow the directions, draw a line along the path to show where you have walked.

Begin at the eastern end of the path. Walk along the path to the nearest pond. Draw an X through it. On the line below this paragraph, suggest something to build here instead of a pond.

_____

Next, follow the path to the flower garden. Suggest some kinds of flowers the queen might like to plant here. Write your suggestions below.

_____

Follow the path to the southernmost bench. Add another bench so that more people can sit here. Finally, go to the fountain. This fountain uses too much water. Draw an X through the fountain.

Try this with a partner. Take turns being blindfolded and following the directions given by your partner. The directions might involve walking across the room, writing on the board, touching your toes, taking three steps forward and five steps back, and so on.

Name_____

Play ball! Decide which word on the baseball diamond answers each clue. Then write the word on the bat that has the same number as the clue.

innings

Signaled   shortstop   grounder   single

fouls

strike   envy

1. This is a one-base hit.

2. A baseball game usually lasts nine of these.

3. This player stands between second base and third base.

4. This word means "jealousy."

5. When the batter swung and missed, the umpire called it this.

6. These balls are hit outside fair territory.

7. If a ball you hit rolls along the grass, you have hit one of these.

8. The coach did this to tell the runner to steal a base.

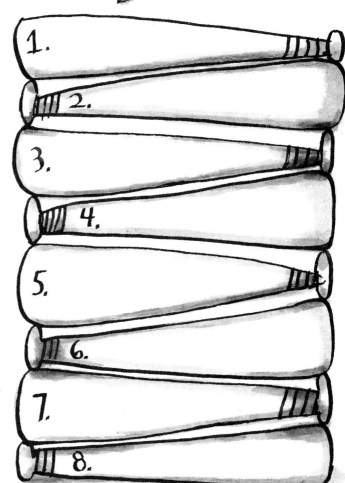

1.
2.
3.
4.
5.
6.
7.
8.

ACTIVITY CORNER

With some classmates, make a Baseball Word Wall. Cut baseball pictures and words from the sports sections of newspapers. Display them on a large poster.

SHORTSTOP FROM TOKYO

Name_____

Complete this character map about Stogie.

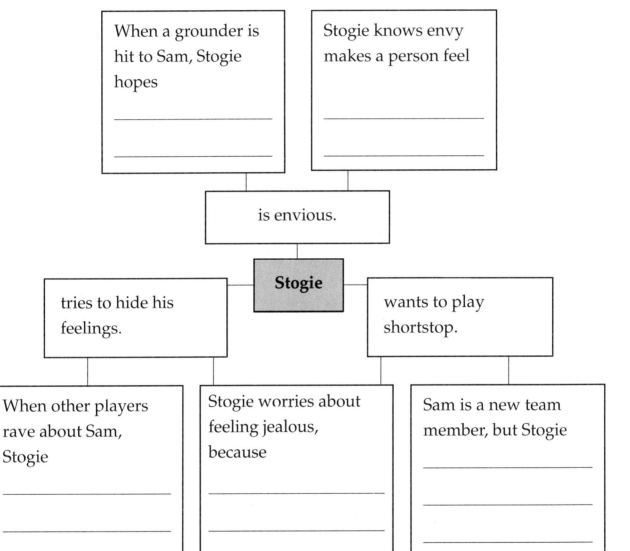

When a grounder is hit to Sam, Stogie hopes

_____

_____

Stogie knows envy makes a person feel

_____

_____

is envious.

Stogie

tries to hide his feelings.

wants to play shortstop.

When other players rave about Sam, Stogie

_____

_____

Stogie worries about feeling jealous, because

_____

_____

Sam is a new team member, but Stogie

_____

_____

_____

Stogie is teased about

_____

_____

Name_____

A. Read the paragraph below and underline each title.

    I read the book *Baseball for Beginners* when I wanted to learn how to play baseball. It must be a good book because soon I was on a team. My teammates made up a silly song about me called "The Kooky Rookie" that told about my many amazing hits and catches. The team was very good. We reached the championship game, which was televised on the program *This Week in Baseball.* The best part was that we won!

B. Rewrite each sentence below. Capitalize and punctuate the titles correctly.

the boys of summer is a book that tells about a famous baseball team.

_____

Robert Francis wrote a poem called the base stealer that tells about someone stealing a base.

_____

_____

On the line below, write a sentence about a book, poem, or story. Be sure to include the title.

_____

SUMMARIZING *the* **L**EARNING Capitalize the _____, _____, and the important words in a title. Use _____ for a story, a poem, or a song. _____ the title of a book, a magazine, or a T.V. show.

••• SHORTSTOP FROM TOKYO •••

Name_____

Write *opinion* or *fact* to describe what each player is saying.

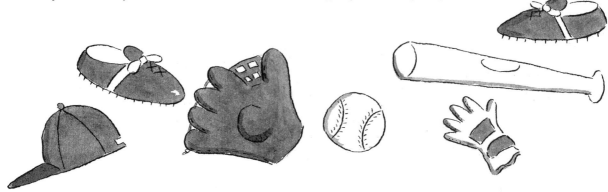

Catcher:	Our team is winning.	_____
Pitcher:	The umpire is awful.	_____
First baseman:	It's a perfect day for baseball.	_____
Second baseman:	The sun is shining.	_____
Third baseman:	It's too hot.	_____
Shortstop:	I have a new glove.	_____
Left fielder:	The stands are full.	_____
Center fielder:	The crowd is too noisy.	_____
Right fielder:	This is a great game.	_____
Batter:	We'll beat this team easily.	_____

ACTIVITY CORNER

Choose a famous athlete, and make a fact-and-opinion chart about him or her. With a partner, find information about the person from several sources, such as newspapers, magazines, and television reports. List facts and opinions on a large chart, and tell the source for each. Feel free to add your own opinions.

••• SHORTSTOP FROM TOKYO •••

Name _____

A. Read each question below. After it, write *dictionary* or *encyclopedia* to tell where you would find the information.

1. What is the correct pronunciation of *stadium*? _____

2. How old is Fenway Park in Boston? _____

3. What is the major industry in Flint, Michigan? _____

4. What does *artificial* mean? _____

5. Who invented the first artificial limb, and when was it first used?

   _____

6. How has the design of baseball bats changed over the years?

   _____

7. Who are some of the most famous players in baseball history?

   _____

B. Choose one of the topics below. Use a dictionary and an encyclopedia to research the topic. Then write about what you find in each reference source.

baseball	football	tennis
soccer	basketball	volleyball

Dictionary entry: _____

_____

Encyclopedia entry: _____

_____

Name _____

Read the following paragraph. Use clues in the story to determine the meaning of the underlined words. Then write each word on the line next to its meaning.

    I heard the clattering of <u>hooves</u> on the hard dirt road long before I saw the horses. The two <u>gauchos</u> got off their horses and welcomed me to the ranch. They asked me what kind of work I wanted to do. I told them that I would be good at feeding the horses and brushing their <u>manes</u>. The gauchos looked at each other, and one of them asked me if I could use a <u>lasso</u> to capture a runaway horse. The other asked me if I would be able to put a <u>brand</u> on the three new horses they had brought back with them. I had the feeling that after a relaxing <u>siesta</u> in the shade, my adventure in Argentina was about to begin.

1. _____ a mark made on an animal with a hot iron

2. _____ cowhands of the South American pampas

3. _____ long hair on the neck of some animals

4. _____ afternoon nap

5. _____ long rope with a loop at the end

6. _____ hard coverings on the feet of some animals

Name _____

A. One way to summarize a nonfiction selection is to complete a K-W-L chart. Use the one below before, during, and after reading.

K *What I Know*	W *What I Want to Know*	L *What I Learned*

B. Write a one-sentence summary about the selection.

_____

_____

Name_____

A. Read the paragraph below. Underline all the abbreviations.

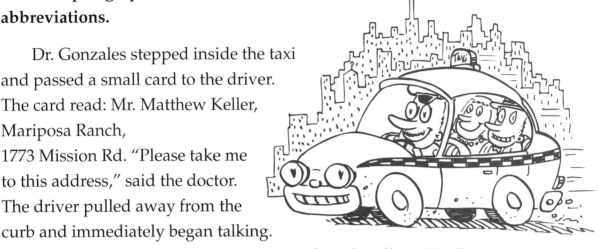

Dr. Gonzales stepped inside the taxi and passed a small card to the driver. The card read: Mr. Matthew Keller, Mariposa Ranch, 1773 Mission Rd. "Please take me to this address," said the doctor. The driver pulled away from the curb and immediately began talking.

"My name is Juan Rodríguez, but my friends call me J.R.," he began.

B. Rewrite the following items using abbreviations.

Mister William Torres   _____

345 Bacon Ranch Road   _____

Born: January 3, 1945   _____

Married: February 9, 1970   _____

Write the month, date, and day of the week of your birthday on the line below. Use abbreviations where you can.

_____

SUMMARIZING

the **L**EARNING   Shortened forms of words are called _____.

Most abbreviations end with a _____. Abbreviations of proper nouns

begin with a _____.

Name _____

A. Read the following paragraph. Decide which sentences in it are facts and which are opinions. Then write the number of each sentence in the appropriate place on the chart.

    (1) Buenos Aires is a very interesting city. (2) It is the capital of Argentina. (3) Argentina is the second-largest country in South America, after Brazil. (4) Buenos Aires is located in eastern Argentina, near Uruguay. (5) It is Argentina's chief port and cultural center. (6) If you live in Argentina and you don't live in Buenos Aires, you should move. (7) If you live in, for example, Santiago, you really should consider moving to Buenos Aires. (8) There are many more interesting things to do and see in Buenos Aires than in any other city in Argentina.

Facts	Opinions
_____	_____

B. On the line before each sentence, write *F* if the statement is a fact or *O* if the statement is an opinion.

_____ 1. Susanita lived at the estancia year-round.

_____ 2. It's better to live on a ranch than in a city.

_____ 3. Susanita had her own horse.

_____ 4. The horse María finally got was better than Susanita's.

_____ 5. Swimming in the creek on a horse was great fun.

_____ 6. Carbonada is a thick stew made of corn and peaches.

_____ 7. A ñandú egg is so big that it supplies all the egg needed for a whole cake.

Name _____

A. Read each of the sentences below. On the line, write what
   is being compared.

1. Students in Argentina usually get the summer off, as do

   students in the United States. _____

   _____

2. Grandma, like María, had been working hard all morning

   cooking lunch. _____

3. The oil fields in Argentina produce almost all the country's

   oil, and they provide natural gas, too. _____

   _____

B. Read each of the sentences below. On the line, write what
   is being contrasted.

1. Pampita wasn't a very fast horse, but Salguero's horse was quick.

   _____

2. Susanita was always ready for an adventure. María, however, was

   sometimes afraid. _____

3. On one hand, the grown-ups wanted a siesta after lunch. On the other

   hand, Susanita and María wanted to do things. _____

   _____

••• ON THE PAMPAS •••

Name_____

Use the map to answer the questions.

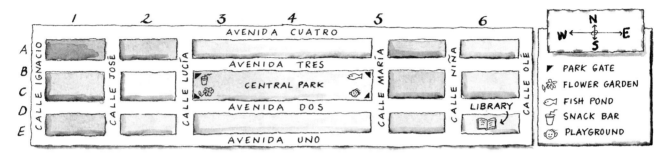

1. Imagine that you are at the northeast entrance of the park.
Which park attraction is closest to you?

_____

2. Imagine that you are at the southwest entrance of the park.
You want to get to the corner of Calle Ignacio and Avenida
Cuatro. Use a marker to trace the path on the map. Then
write the directions on the lines below.

_____

_____

_____

3. What building can you find in the area E-6?

_____

4. Put a red X at the northeast corner of Avenida Cuatro and Calle Olé.

Draw a map of a park you'd like to have in your neighborhood. Share your
ideas with a classmate. Explain why each part of your park would be a good
addition to your neighborhood.

SKILLS AND STRATEGIES INDEX